PRA
HOW TO H

"This book addresses one of the biggest challenges of leadership: how to hold on to your humanity while maintaining empathy for those you lead, all while meeting your bottom line. Written with clarity and warmth, the book shares best practices through powerful examples and transformative easy-to-access exercises."

—NIR EYAL, author of *Hooked* and *Indistractable*

"Perfectly timed and necessary reading for today's leaders, *How to Hold Power* is filled with inspiring insights, stories, and practical exercises to implement right away. Reading this book feels like Pavini Moray is sitting calmly beside you, ushering you on a journey to becoming a more grounded, impactful, and sought-out leader. Highly recommend this book!"

—CARRIE MELISSA JONES, community builder, entrepreneur, and community management consultant

"This book offers a roadmap to becoming a leader that people love. Weaving experiential practice with hard-won insight, Pavini has written a book that will be indispensable for anyone who wants to lead in a powerful, embodied way."

—DAVID TRELEAVEN, PhD, author of *Trauma-Sensitive Mindfulness*

"Drawing from decades of experience in somatics, Pavini breaks leadership down into its most essential components: boundaries, consent, and listening. Chock-full of effective and practical suggestions for how to deal with workplace triggers and conflict, *How to Hold Power* will help you develop a meaningful leadership practice. Filled with compassion and wisdom, this is a must-read book for every leader who wants to hold their power with skills and grace."

—BECKY MARGIOTTA, author of *Impact with Integrity* and cofounder of the Billions Institute

"Pavini offers a unique voice in the world of embodied leadership. They can only be described as one who has great courage and has worked hard to accomplish and realize what it means to be embodied in truth and wholeness. Breaking down a system to understand how to realize this is an invaluable offering to the world at a time when it is deeply needed."

—LUCIA HORAN, 5Rhythms Lineage holder and
Executive Somatic Coach

"*How to Hold Power* is a remarkable book. In it, Pavini Moray is compassionate about the pressures those in positions of leadership face, having lived those pressures, while at the same time holding those leaders to a high standard. The book shows how a path of development based on connecting to our sensations and emotions allows us to be better bosses. In addition, it remains practical and grounded and provides leaders a set of practices to be the bosses they aspire to be. It is a must-read!"

—PETE HAMILL, PhD, senior teacher at Strozzi
Institute and founder of Uncommon Leaders Ltd

"*How to Hold Power* is a practical and invaluable guide that is accessible, down-to-earth, insightful, and honest. It will help readers transform the way they lead and the way they live their lives. As a yoga studio owner and yoga teacher, so much of what Pavini writes resonates with me in terms of what I teach: I encourage students to drop out of their thinking minds and into their feeling bodies and remind them to listen to the wisdom of their bodies. I remind them not to believe everything they think, as those narratives and stories are quite often untrue and almost always limiting. I encourage them to cultivate mindfulness and to move and breathe with awareness and intention. If you are ready to rethink your relationship to leadership and power, to lead with compassion and empathy, to strengthen your communication and listening skills, and to work on creating and honoring boundaries, read this book, work through its exercises, and be ready to become a boss or leader that inspires others."

—JENNIFER LENHART, owner and lead teacher at
Satsang Yoga Studio, Berea, Ohio

"With a balance of personal stories, humor, and notes on somatic leadership, Pavini Moray delivers an easy-to-read book that will benefit a wide range of folks at every level of leadership."

—MEREDITH BROOME, Master Somatic Coach

"Many successful entrepreneurs are masters of disassociation—unconsciously setting aside our own needs and feelings to get stuff done. In this brilliant debut, Dr. Moray makes a compelling case for bosses to pause, reflect on, and process our own (often uncomfortable) feelings so that we can show up for the people around us with clarity and grace.

By combining content with real-time practices, Dr. Moray lays out an easy-to-follow roadmap that guides the reader on a journey of self-awareness, self-acceptance, and finally, self-leadership—skills that any boss must master before they can lead others.

How to Hold Power is sure to become an essential resource for any boss who wants to pursue personal growth toward more conscious leadership."

—MICHELLE COYLE, president of BGSD Strategies

"Reading *How to Hold Power*, I kept coming back to one overwhelming thought: how I wish I'd had this book decades ago! It's full of wisdom, insight, and practices that will be invaluable not just for managers but for anyone taking leadership in an organization or finding themself in a position of influence in a group. Moray's metaphor of the dragon tail—the extra weight and impact your words have when you take up a position of authority—alone would have saved me many challenging conflicts! I look forward to using these teachings and will recommend the book to my students and trainees."

—STARHAWK, author, activist, permaculture designer, and teacher

"The opportunity to make work mean more than product and payment now has a blueprint. Dr. Pavini Moray has crafted a mind- and heart-opening journey of discovery for anyone in the world of work and beyond. *How to Hold Power* belongs alongside all of your best business and management books, and by your bedside. For the business leader, you will get immediate practices that open avenues of empathy and vision. For visionaries, you will find delightful pathways to patience, presence, and perseverance. This book's time has come. If you find it in your hands, you will find in yourself a new leader—in the moment, embodied."

—STEVEN HOSKINSON, founder of Organic Intelligence

HOW

TO

HOLD

POWER

HOW TO HOLD POWER

A Somatic Approach *to* Becoming *a* Leader People Love *and* Respect

PAVINI MORAY, PhD

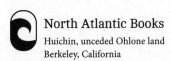

North Atlantic Books
Huichin, unceded Ohlone land
Berkeley, California

Published by
North Atlantic Books
Huichin, unceded Ohlone land
Berkeley, California

Cover design by Amanda Weiss
Book design by Happenstance Type-O-Rama

Printed in the United States of America

How to Hold Power: A Somatic Approach to Becoming a Leader People Love and Respect is sponsored and published by North Atlantic Books, an educational nonprofit based in the unceded Ohlone land Huichin (Berkeley, CA) that collaborates with partners to develop cross-cultural perspectives; nurture holistic views of art, science, the humanities, and healing; and seed personal and global transformation by publishing work on the relationship of body, spirit, and nature.

North Atlantic Books's publications are distributed to the US trade and internationally by Penguin Random House Publisher Services. For further information, visit our website at *www.northatlanticbooks.com.*

Library of Congress Cataloging-in-Publication Data
Names: Moray, Pavini, author.
Title: How to hold power : a somatic approach to becoming a leader people
    love and respect / Pavini Moray, PhD.
Description: Berkeley, CA : North Atlantic Books, 2023. | Includes
    bibliographical references and index. | Summary: "A guide to becoming a
    better boss that discusses how to support your team, dismantle toxic
    work culture, and lead with integrity"-- Provided by publisher.
Identifiers: LCCN 2023013573 (print) | LCCN 2023013574 (ebook) | ISBN
    9781623179243 (trade paperback) | ISBN 9781623179250 (ebook)
Subjects: LCSH: Leadership--Psychological aspects. | Mind and body. | Self.
Classification: LCC BF637.L4 M67 2023 (print) | LCC BF637.L4 (ebook) |
    DDC 158/.4--dc23/eng/20230614
LC record available at https://lccn.loc.gov/2023013573
LC ebook record available at https://lccn.loc.gov/2023013574

1 2 3 4 5 6 7 8 9 KPC 27 26 25 24 23

This book includes recycled material and material from well-managed forests. North Atlantic Books is committed to the protection of our environment. We print on recycled paper whenever possible and partner with printers who strive to use environmentally responsible practices.

CONTENTS

INTRODUCTION

MANY BOSSES I TALK with project confidence, but behind closed doors they express fear, anxiety, and stress. Perhaps you, too, have made great personal sacrifices to get your business or organization off the ground and are struggling to keep going in the wake of unexpected disaster. Maybe you're determined to be a leader whom people respect, but you also struggle with a desire to be liked. Maybe you doubt that you're strong enough to see your organization through the storm without abandoning ship. Maybe you've given up your time, your friendships, your money, your relationships, and even your mental and physical health, all to do a good job—but now what?

Your job is demanding and humbling, and I'm guessing your work landscape is also in a dramatic state of flux. Around the globe and across industries, expectations and rules for work that had felt solid for years are now being called into question. Since the COVID-19 pandemic, employees have left their jobs in droves, desiring more personal gratification and autonomy. Bosses are realizing the power employees have—including power that can get bosses fired. Concepts of authority and hierarchy in the workplace are shifting, and values of equity and social justice are becoming priorities. As a boss today, you have woken up to a new and very different world. No one likes feeling as if they don't understand the rules or that the rules have shifted. The conventional wisdom of work has changed, and you need new skills to navigate a new reality.

For instance, many bosses I've spoken with are afraid of being "canceled." They worry about their words and actions costing them their careers.

When conflict comes up at work, many bosses feel like they're walking on eggshells; they want to say and do the right thing, but they aren't always sure what the right thing is. Fear is costing companies bucketloads of money as fearful bosses stifle their leadership instincts, leading to communication failures, and employees are left without solid boundaries and guidance.

Understanding the new rules will require *all* of you, not just your mind. To make this change, you will have to learn to *be* in a very different way. If you want to get different results, you need to do something different from what you've been doing. That's why you're here: to find out how.

Who This Book Is For

This book is for managers, directors, founders, entrepreneurs, and bosses of all kinds who want to lead their teams skillfully. You want empowered employees who display ownership over their work. You want your team to follow your leadership with minimal friction. If this is you, you're in the right place. This book will help you learn how to embody your power, have thriving relationships in the workplace, and lead your team with clarity and confidence.

My guess is that you're reading this because you want to inhabit your leadership differently. You may be a new boss, just learning to lead. Or you may have been a boss for a while and are looking for more effective leadership tools.

When you're considering any significant change, the future can feel distant and unobtainable. You may know precisely what you want, but you don't have the map. You need a plan, a structure, and specific steps that will lead you to where you want to be.

But before you can develop this plan, you need to start by asking yourself these important—and sometimes difficult—questions:

- How do I feel about the people I manage?
- How do they feel about me?
- How is stress affecting my physical and mental health?
- How is my family affected by my work stress and anxiety?
- How do I feel about my leadership?

- Do I feel free and inspired at work?
- Or am I awash in worry and tension, with a constant undercurrent of fear?

These are serious questions because stress has a severe impact on your health. Professional burnout is no joke. Leadership can be hazardous to your health. Holding power is complicated, and we have so few models for how to do it effectively and sustainably. You'll need to do and be different if you want leadership to be more easeful.

In this book, you'll learn how sustainable change comes from body-based practice, rather than your head; you can't change things by thinking alone! To create change that lasts, you've got to change three things: your stories, your practices, and how you live inside your body. This is the goal of the work we'll do together in this book—changing how you live in your body and how you relate in your relationships.

Who Am I, and Why Should You Listen to Me?

This book comes from my own story of becoming a boss, fraught with trials and tribulations along the way. After a dozen-plus years as a somatic coach, I had worked with thousands of clients and students, guiding them to live more embodied lives and create thriving relationships. I had a good handle on what worked. With a master's degree in educational design and a PhD in somatic psychology, I founded an educational tech startup teaching relationship skills to the masses. The problem was, I'd never led a company before.

My path to becoming a boss was arduous. As a queer and trans founder, I found few role models of corporate leaders who practiced in accordance with my social justice beliefs. There were scant resources to help me understand how to hold my power without causing harm. While becoming a leader, I made many costly and painful mistakes.

After years of doing everything myself, I suddenly had employees. People's careers and livelihoods were now my responsibility. I had a team turning to me to make all the important decisions. They had feelings and feedback about my leadership. I was financially, emotionally, and ethically responsible for all my company's choices. I had power that I didn't quite want and didn't know how to use appropriately.

Wasn't it good enough to treat my employees like I wanted to be treated? I quickly found that it wasn't! We all struggled while I tried to navigate my new power. It took time to truly feel my position and recognize my impact. A core component of this process was learning how to embody my strength responsibly instead of harming my employees by insisting I was one of them. I had to develop the body of a leader.

How do I know it's worth it to become embodied? I recently read a list titled something like "Twenty-Six Mistakes New Bosses Make" and I cringed with every item. *Ouch.* For every new detail on that list, I was like, "Yeah, I've done that." *Oof.* Being embodied certainly didn't save me from making uninformed newbie mistakes.

But you know what happened next? I got to the end of that list, and I thought, "Yep, being a boss is hard." Here's where my embodiment saved me. I didn't feel bad. I didn't hate myself. I honored the truth that I am human. I acknowledged my attempt to lead others with skill, compassion, grace, and courage. My embodied self could roll with making mistakes—without being unkind to myself. That's what I want for you: healthy pride and self-compassion.

In this book, you can learn from my (way more than) twenty-six mistakes. I want to help you feel into your work life and your boss self with freedom, ease, and joy. Together we'll explore who you want to be as a boss. We'll figure out how to get you there using the tools of embodiment and expanded relationship skills. By the end of this process, you'll be a boss who feels and relates with skill.

What You Will Learn

Many leadership and management books tell you what to do once you become a boss, but very few help you *feel* like a leader. In an informal survey of over two dozen leadership books, I found only *three* pages acknowledging that leaders are people with bodies. Three pages! Those pages were all about body language, i.e., *Don't fold your arms in front of you if you want to have an open conversation.* Oh, you don't say? You need, and deserve, more than that.

My goal is to offer you pragmatic advice and effective practices enabling you to be a stellar boss and to develop your embodied leadership presence. This book brings human-centric, consent-based, trauma-informed approaches to guide you through a process of personal transformation to create just and equitable workplaces.

THIS BOOK HAS TWO SIMPLE PREMISES:

1. Your power as a boss comes from inside you. You connect with it by becoming embodied. Living inside your body helps you be a better human, making you a better leader. Becoming mindful of the emotions and sensations inside your body benefits your leadership by giving you access to more information.

2. As a leader, you need good people skills. You can continuously improve because relationship skills are learnable. Boundaries, consent, and listening are the three-legged stool of good leadership.

In other words, if you want to be a leader people love to work with, get good at feeling yourself and relating with skill.

Your leadership does not arrive with your job title. Your leadership comes when you become a body your employees wish to follow. The qualities of how you live in your body determine your leadership—your presence, your groundedness, your ability to listen, your capacity to be with complexity, your ability to communicate with clarity, your decisive action. These are the qualities of leadership that inspire people to follow your suggestions. Your body will be there on your leadership journey, every moment of the way. It can become a trusted ally and advisor if you learn to trust the wisdom it offers.

Many people think that work is a separate part of their life. But this kind of compartmentalized thinking leads to the fragmentation and depersonalization that is at the core of so many toxic work environments. You *can* be an integrated and whole person, both at home and at work. Wherever you go, you take your body with you. The skills and practices that positively affect your work life will benefit your entire life. Becoming embodied as a boss means becoming represented as a human. Although this book was written for bosses who want a new way to lead, it can help you level up your entire life.

The book is organized into two parts. Part I focuses on inhabiting your somatic self, and part II focuses on embodied leadership in action. You may be surprised to find little mention of leadership and work in part I. This is intentional, so stick with me! Somatic work is whole-self work, so it is important to start with who you are in *all* areas of your life. After all, you bring your whole self to the workplace—whether you want to or not.

In chapter 1, you'll learn the basic principle of somatics, the first of which is: you have a body! As obvious as this may seem, it's something we too often forget. We'll be working with different parts of your somatic experience in this book, including your physical body, the stories you believe to be true about the world, and what you choose to practice. You'll learn that to create sustained change in your leadership, you must change all three of these parts of your body.

Chapter 2 explores why feeling your inner experience is valuable as a leader. Leaders who can access their internal wisdom and embody their leadership presence tend to make better decisions.

You know that tension you hold in your body? That's where we head in chapter 3, as you learn about muscle contractions and how they take care of you. You'll learn how to work with your contractions to feel more freedom.

In chapter 4 we dive into how to feel yourself. This is where you will relearn to feel your sensations and emotions. When you can feel the information coming from your body, you can make wise choices. This chapter explores the foundational practices for embodiment.

Part II begins by heading into the arena of power in chapter 5. You'll learn more about the different types of power and how you feel them. Feeling your power is the fast track to leading others with skill and grace.

Chapter 6 helps you develop an embodiment practice at work. You'll learn how to easily weave mindful somatic practice into your day, so you can feel grounded and present while working.

Chapter 7 takes you into the terrain of triggers and how you can work with them. Creating a trauma-informed workplace supports your workers in feeling safe. You'll learn how to navigate times when you or your employee gets activated at work.

There are three essential skills you must have to be a leader people love: having and honoring boundaries, practicing consent, and listening effectively. Chapters 8–10 will break these important concepts down so you can integrate them into your leadership.

Chapter 11 tackles workplace conflict and how you can train as an ethical fighter. You'll learn what to do during conflict and, more importantly, how to repair in a way that builds trust.

In chapter 12, you'll put it all together to create a culture of embodied humanity in your workplace.

How to Use This Book

This book is, above all, a somatic learning tool. I will share some of the theory behind somatics as background, but the primary goal is to learn to be inside your skin differently. In general, somatics (the study of the body's wisdom) is more relatable through examples than through theory, so I will be sharing stories as we go. All stories have had identifying information changed. Some are composites of multiple clients to protect client identities further.

Even more than reading stories, somatics is most powerfully learned through *doing*. This book offers you a transformative process that will be uniquely yours. It will help if you read it in the order presented because the skill sequence builds on itself. Go slow and take time to absorb the information. Stick with it, especially when things are uncomfortable. Please know that I'm writing from a place of deep love and respect, and that all feelings are valid. The moments when we are most uncomfortable are often the times when we learn the most—as long as we stay open and willing.

As you read, you'll come across sections titled "Practice Moment." Do these exercises when you read them. Most of them take just a minute or two. Don't skip them, thinking, "Oh, I'll come back and do that later." Do them now. You'll need to have either a notebook or a document to write your answers to some of the practices.

This book can only help you if you practice. To set you up for success, I suggest that the first time you do a practice, do it exactly as I describe. As you become more familiar with the practices and begin to develop your somatic awareness, you can tweak the exercises to align with your needs and curiosities.

For the practice moments, it helps if you are in a space where you can give your full focus. Each practice will have specific instructions, but in general, being present helps. You can close your eyes or keep them open.

Learning to live in your body is a lifelong practice. Although you can return to any of the practices presented at any time—and you'll get more benefit from repetition—it's important to know that your intuition is crucial. Don't do a practice because you are "supposed to." These practices are intended to be useful to you in your leadership journey, but over time you will find that what you need and want to practice will shift. This is normal. Almost no practice is the right practice forever. As you change and grow, so do your practices.

This book is about the wisdom of your sensations and emotions, and your body's understanding. So let's invite your body to this party!

PRACTICE MOMENT: Noticing Yourself

Your inner experience is vast, wealthy, and so wise. Take a moment now and notice:

- What do you feel as you read this?
- Are you excited? Scared?
- Can you feel your heart beating?
- Is your stomach digesting?
- What else are you noticing in your body?

PART I

INHABITING

YOUR

SOMATIC

SELF

1

YOU HAVE A BODY!

ON THE COAST of the Pacific Ocean in Northern California, gnarly old cypress trees grow. Their misshapen roots cling fiercely to the western edge of the North American continent. Their twisted limbs are shaped by the wind constantly blowing inland from the sea. Looking at them, you can see how the constant wind pressure has sculpted their bodies. They dig into a crumbling edge of land to keep from tumbling down hundreds of feet and crashing into the ocean below. Their thick, scarred bark has to withstand unrelenting weather and salt spray. Their branches hang low, wider at the bottom, while their outlines shrink into smaller, narrower shapes higher up. The climate they live in is dry, with sparse annual rainfall. When the rain finally comes, it comes in torrents. The tree roots must be deep enough to hold on through gale-force winds, storms, and mudslides. The roots must also be broad and porous to absorb enough nutrients to survive the entire year.

The same tree in another environment would look very different. The bodies and survival strategies of cypress trees are unique and specialized to their bioregion, and have been shaped by their environment. Like these trees, your body is also determined by the internal and external forces you experience. You are shaped by the environment you live in, the survival strategies you employ, and your experiences.

Soma comes from a Greek root word meaning "body." You have a body that is *you*. Somatics is the study of the first-person internal perception of the human body. That's a fancy way to say that somatics studies how you place attention in your inner experience. Your somatic experience is what you notice and feel inside yourself.

Three Essential Parts of Your Somatic Body

1. Your **physical body** includes your bones, organs, and systems. It also includes your survival responses, emotions, and sensations. Included are your internal muscular contractions and how the forces in your life have physically shaped you. You talk about your body like this: "I am hungry." "I feel happy." "My leg hurts." In other words, talking about your body involves talking about what you feel and experience.

2. Your **narratives** are the stories you believe to be true about yourself, life, and the world. These are your beliefs, mindsets, and values that are inseparable from you. You talk about your narratives like this: "I am a joyful person." "I am the kind of person who likes to lounge." "I believe time travel is possible." In other words, your narratives are what you believe or think.

3. Your **practices** are the things you *do*. Everything you do is a practice. You talk about your practices like this: "I went to the gym." "I read the news every day." "I go to sleep at nine p.m."

This book will help you become the boss you want to be by asking you to examine these three parts of your somatic body. Each of these parts of your somatic body is important in and of itself. The coming together of these elements makes a sum greater than its parts: your unique life.

Like the cypress tree, your life and personality are shaped by external and internal forces, such as your family; your friends; the institutions in which you participate, like schools and religions; the identities you hold; your hobbies and interests; the amount of access you have to resources; how much social privilege you have; and any cultural oppression you experience. You are also shaped by the environment you live in, by the very Earth and water you consume.

When seeking change, working with your body helps get you where you want to be more deeply and effectively. Working through a somatic lens takes the entirety of you into account, not just your psyche, your past, or your future goals. Somatics is the fast track to sustained personal change. You can't just think yourself into being a better boss. You have to change who you are, what you believe, and what you do.

Your Somatic Shape and Impact: Meet Linden

Linden came to me seeking somatic coaching because she felt like she was outside her life. She was having trouble connecting with others, including her coworkers, her children, and her partner. She could see the joy and engagement that others experienced, yet she couldn't feel it for herself. Her life was objectively good—she had enough money, a beautiful home, and a great family. But she was numb, and her life felt empty. She couldn't understand why she felt so hollow when she had everything she was supposed to have.

When Linden walked into my office for the first time, what stood out to me was how tightly she held her body. She didn't sit; she perched. Every muscle was tensed through our early meetings, as if she was about to jump. As I sat with her, my body responded to hers. I noticed how my breathing grew shallower and how tired my body felt. I knew Linden craved more freedom, but another part of her was hell-bent on holding it all together.

Her upper body was rigid. She sucked her stomach inward. When she walked, her gait was stiff and inflexible. When we sat together, she rarely met my eyes. She told me she had been a high-performing student and her family had high expectations of her, and she met their expectations through athletics and academics. She had an MBA from a prestigious university and was CFO at an established Bay Area tech firm.

At work, her employees and coworkers found her difficult to be around. It wasn't her competency they questioned, because she did her job to the letter. The feedback she received was that her performance was excellent, but her teamwork was lacking. She didn't know how to share responsibility. Her employees felt like she didn't trust them, and she felt responsible for doing everything herself.

Any time I offered Linden feedback, a strange thing happened. She would listen, then say "yes," and bounce onto another topic. Anything I provided, any below-the-surface questions I asked, all bounced off of her, like a hard rubber ball rebounding off a wall. Her protective layer prevented her from experiencing the closeness she wanted. It was also preventing her from being an effective boss because she repelled her team's suggestions and feedback the same way she did mine.

Linden had developed a somatic body that would not receive impact. Watching her struggle to receive anything at all was heartbreaking. Nothing anyone offered her, good or bad, could touch her. She felt agonizingly alone. My heart hurt being in her presence. Here was this woman who seemingly had it all but who couldn't feel a thing.

It took a long time for Linden to be able to feel her protection. I began gently directing her attention to it when the bounce would happen. She would blink rapidly and be surprised. Even when she was discussing challenging topics, such as difficult feedback, her child's struggles, or her aging and controlling mother, she couldn't feel the impact of any of it.

To help Linden feel the impact, I made a soft ball out of cloth. We practiced by standing in my office, and I would say a statement like, "Mommy, I am scared," and toss the ball at Linden, lightly hitting her torso. The first few times we did this practice, she felt baffled. The sensation of physical impact was unfamiliar to her. The ball would fall to the floor, and she wouldn't react at all. Then I asked her to notice her emotions. After a few more rounds with the statement and the ball's impact, she began to feel something, but she couldn't name it. After every practice round, we discussed what we both noticed. Linden gradually became aware of how she always braced for impact. She described the bracing as "constantly being under a barrage."

Once she could feel the bracing, we turned toward helping her learn to receive. In one session, she arrived in my office after she had gone to the doctor for her annual physical exam. She beamed as she entered and told me she had figured it out! She knew how to receive. "You know those little doors in the bathroom at the doctor, where you slide your pee cup in, and then on the other side, there's another door, and they take it out? That's how I can receive!"

She found a way to embody this image that allowed her to receive impact on her own timetable. Little by little, she allowed herself to feel. She knew how to put the rubber shell on when needed, so she could let a little door exist within it. Linden had discovered an essential somatic truth: she needed time to be able to receive. The impact could present itself to her exterior and then hang out in the middle section for a bit; and then, when she was ready, she could open her internal door and feel it.

Linden learned that she could sometimes soften. She could allow herself to be impacted by something someone shared with her. She started to allow herself to let in a little bit more of the world. We worked on a way to name this new shape. The narrative she came up with was "I am receptive to the goodwill of others."

As we continued to work somatically, she found new ways to practice being at work. She discovered that engaging her hard rubber shell and telling herself she was receptive didn't work. She had to learn to be inside her body in a new way. She had to create alignment between her narrative and her body.

At work, she began a practice of settling back in her chair when her employees would come to speak with her. She practiced feeling her back against the chair. She practiced listening for meaning. She practiced allowing information to come in and allowing herself to feel moved by it.

Linden created a new somatic body for herself. As she did, she found her work relationships thriving. She started to feel closer with others outside of work. She could feel her love for her kids and her partner, a little bit at a time. Although she could still put up her protective shell when needed, she found she preferred to receive the goodwill of others.

She became a better boss by changing her somatic shape, practices, and narratives. And she felt happier! Linden was finally able to allow herself to be loved, to give love, and to share her true self with others. It took much work, but the last time she entered my office, her body was open and available. She rested back against the couch and settled. She met my eyes, and I felt her presence. She had changed.

Somatic Change

You are embarking on a path of embodied transformation. Though everyone's journey will be unique to them, somatic change is a systematic and predictable process that has four specific steps: awareness, choice, practice, and integration, in that order.

1. **Awareness:** You become aware of your narratives. Aware of what you are practicing. Aware of how you exist in your body.

2. **Choice:** You consciously choose new narratives. You decide where and how to place your attention. You choose new practices.

3. **Practice:** You practice new ways of being in your body. You practice new habits. You practice new mindsets. You practice new narratives.

4. **Integration:** With practice over time, this change becomes an integrated part of you.

During the entire process of change, you become aware of more and more—more of your narratives, your body, and your practices—and each of these different aspects of awareness contributes to the four steps named above.

Narrative awareness begins as you notice the stories you have told yourself or have been told about yourself that you believe to be true. For example, Linden came to see that the primary narrative in her life was "people can't be trusted." After seeing how that narrative drove most of her interactions, she wanted a different story.

Body awareness begins as you remember that you have a body below your neck. You learn to bring your attention to the world of sensation and emotion within. You become familiar with your survival responses and relearn how to feel. This helps you develop a relationship of trust with your body. Your body responds by providing you with more information that helps you make good decisions.

Practice awareness helps you gain access to more choices. You get to choose new practices that support the change you're making. Linden decided she wanted to practice opening up more to her team.

Narratives

Your narratives are the stories you believe about how you and the world are. You embody your narratives. They live inside you. They are not objective truth, but you experience them as if they are. Your narratives define your experience and the meaning you give to it.

Individuals have narratives. So do families and any grouping of people. For example, is there a black sheep in your family? That's a family narrative. Have you ever believed something about yourself that wasn't true? For example, do you believe "I am lazy," only to watch yourself accomplish massive things? That's a personal narrative. Narratives define your experience, but the stories they tell are not objective reality.

The great news is that narratives are flexible. You can change the stories you believe. You can change what you think about yourself and the world.

You embody many narratives that you have never questioned. You believe them to be accurate or just the way things are. Only when you become aware of your narratives can you change them. One way to become aware of the narratives you hold is to investigate and question your ideas of what you are supposed to be.

PRACTICE MOMENT: Explore Your Narratives

For this practice, you will think about the following questions, and then write down your answers. This is meant to be a fairly brief exercise that should take no more than fifteen minutes or so to complete. Feel free to skip any questions that don't speak to you. Write down the very first thought that comes to your mind as you consider how people like you are supposed to be in the world. Remember, we're not talking about how you actually are. This exercise is intended to help you become aware of the narratives you hold in your body about how you are supposed to be, according to your mindset. Just write whatever words come to mind; there's no need to form complete sentences.

- How are you supposed to look physically?
- How are you supposed to feel emotionally?
- What are you supposed to be able to do?
- What job are you supposed to have?
- How much money are you supposed to make/have?
- What is your primary love relationship supposed to be?
- What is your partner supposed to do/be/look like?
- What kind of house are you supposed to live in?
- What kind of clothes are you supposed to wear?
- Are you supposed to have children, and how are you supposed to raise them?
- What neighborhood should you live in?
- What religion should you practice, and how?
- What is expected with regard to your education?
- What are the rules, values, and beliefs you should live by?

Now that you have answered these questions, put a star next to the narratives you agree with, and draw a line through those you disagree with. Circle any that you are unsure about. Once you become aware of your narratives, you can start to shift them, which will happen later in the book.

The "Shoulds" That Shape You

These "supposed tos" or "shoulds" are external forces that shape what you believe and how you live. "Someone like me should go to college." "Someone like me should play basketball." "Someone like me doesn't get to play hockey." The shoulds become your embodied beliefs or narratives. Once you start to see your narratives, you begin to have more choices about how you respond to them. Later in this chapter, you'll be asked to brainstorm some new narratives for yourself. But before that, let's look at how old embodied narratives can create harm.

I was a very talkative child. Over and over, people told me, "Don't interrupt," or "Interrupting is rude." This hurt my little-kid feelings because I had so many questions! This was my family's version of "children should be seen and not heard." My curiosity, and my voice, were silenced.

If you hear something enough, you take it in and make it yours. I heard "interrupting is rude" so often that I internalized this value. I made it a part of my body. For years, I never interrupted, even when I should have. Not interrupting kept me safe in many circumstances, but there were also costs, like with every strategy. One of the costs of not interrupting was listening to some messed-up stuff without setting boundaries. Not interrupting meant allowing racist and homophobic conversations to continue in my presence. Not interrupting meant that when I was in groups where speaking freely was the norm, I sat quietly, waiting my turn to speak, and never did.

As a new somatic coach, I would wait patiently for my clients to finish speaking. Interrupting them was rude! But sometimes I would wait beyond the end of our session. They would keep talking, and I would sit there, nodding, growing increasingly anxious because my other clients would be kept waiting—all because I was afraid of interrupting and didn't want to seem disrespectful.

As I grew as a coach, I had to get better at setting boundaries. It wasn't professional to let a client talk past the end of the session. It also wasn't professional to keep other clients waiting. As I studied trauma theory, I learned that retelling traumatic stories over and over is not helpful, and I began to understand that my clients could get lost in their telling of a story. All that talking was actually taking valuable time away from their somatic learning, and staying up in the headspace was a bypass around feeling. I noticed that some clients could talk for an entire hour if I didn't interrupt. They paid me a lot of money, but they weren't getting the value of my guidance. Not interrupting meant I wasn't doing my job to help them become the self they wanted to be.

I had grown up believing the narrative that it was terrible to interrupt, and I was scared of changing. But the cost of that old belief was now too high, and I wasn't willing to pay it anymore. So I had to learn how and when to interrupt. I created a new narrative: "Interrupting can be helpful; not interrupting can be harmful."

The practice of interrupting was a skill I had to learn. For a long time, every time I practiced it, the old narrative would pop up alongside my new routine; but I kept going, trusting in the process. By understanding how I had been socialized, I challenged the belief that it was rude to interrupt. I put a new belief into place, supported by new practices, and I became a better coach.

Do you remember the four steps of somatic change that we discussed earlier? This is one example of how they work in real life. As an adult, I became **aware** of and assessed my belief about interrupting, and I made the **choice** to change it. I figured out a new narrative that I wanted to embody. Then I **practiced** interrupting until I **integrated** both the belief and the practice.

Nowadays, I tell new clients up front that I interrupt with purpose. I gain their consent and assure them that it is okay to let me know if they don't want to be interrupted. When I do interrupt (with consent) I listen to my gut, which tells me when it's the right time. Interrupting has become a vital tool in my coach's toolkit and one my clients tell me they benefit from.

Leading with a Growth Mindset

Your beliefs, narratives, and values exist inside you, guiding your decisions. If you don't investigate them, you're at their mercy. Your limiting beliefs can drive your life if you let them. For a boss, this is dangerous. Becoming aware of who you are and what you believe means you can make conscious choices about who you want to be and how you want to lead.

A growth mindset is crucial, and there are many great books out there on the topic. Having a growth mindset lets you be someone who can learn, who can change, who doesn't have to know everything already. With a growth mindset, you become more comfortable in the mystery of not knowing. In this work, you get to embrace being a beginner. This may seem daunting, and even risky, if you believe that bosses are supposed to know everything already.

The good news is that your brain is incredibly flexible. You have the power to break yourself out of the ruts of conditioned thinking and choose what you want to believe. You can choose to think you are a boss who learns, who can shift and grow and develop. You can believe that your best boss self is continually emerging. That there is no "there" to get to. That leadership is a magical journey. That life is a grand adventure, where you are constantly discovering new parts of yourself, new capacities, and new desires. What possibilities and beauty!

You can only embody what you believe is possible. So get creative—and brave!—by inviting new beliefs about what is possible for your team, your company, and your life.

You get to create your narratives. You get to create your boss mindset. What do you want to believe? Which narratives are you choosing?

PRACTICE MOMENT: Choose Your New Narratives

Grab your writing device. Make a quick list of ten or more things you want to believe as a boss. Here is some inspiration:

- I am a boss who listens.

- I am a boss who balances profit with care.

- I am a boss who trusts my employees to do their job.

- I can bring my whole self to work.

- I can be a boss who loves my employees and has professional boundaries.

- I can be a boss who leads with inspiration.

At the end of this practice, take a moment to reread what you've come up with. What are you sensing inside? Do any of the beliefs you want to adopt scare you? Excite you? Circle any new narratives that feel alive inside of you.

How to Know Your Somatic Body

Becoming acquainted with your somatic body takes time. It is a process of self-reflection in which you must learn to place your attention *inside* your experience. At the same time, you're exploring your narratives and practices and then deciding what you want to embody.

Each of us lives inside our body, from our first breath until our last. From this place, you decide what is normal and acceptable for you. For Linden, living with chronically constricted muscles so that impact and feelings bounced off of her was normal. She didn't know any other way of being.

I can say with confidence that you have at least one habituated and chronic muscle contraction in your body. One way you hear people talk about this is the phrase "where I carry tension." Perhaps your shoulders are perpetually raised toward your ears. Maybe you clench your teeth when you drive. You may pull in your tummy muscles or contract your behind. Each of us has somatic strategies, like contractions, that help us cope with the stresses of life.

Because you don't know any other way of being right now, perceiving your own somatic habits can be tricky. You can't know what you don't know, after all—at least not without help. It can be helpful to work with a somatic coach trained in making bodily assessments, who can track how you hold your breath, how you move and don't move your body, and where you're holding tension. A good coach invites your awareness of these patterns without judgment or shame.

It's important for you to know that these contractions are not wrong or bad. You developed them, most likely at a young age, to take care of yourself. They are protective. They are your safety system. In no way am I suggesting that you get rid of them. Instead, the goal is to learn to work with them so you can have more freedom and choice.

It's never a good idea to dismantle a safety system without deciding how you will stay safe afterward. If you have a burglar alarm in your house, you put it there for security. What would happen if you chose to take it out without installing a new system? You would probably feel incredibly vulnerable, and you might even freak out! Your internal protective systems are similar. However, an important difference is that even if you decide to change your internal protective strategies, they will still be there if you ever need them. So if the thought of making these changes or giving up these particular coping mechanisms makes you nervous, rest assured that you will always have access to these familiar systems.

When you get curious about your somatic body, you start to learn a whole new language of expression. Most people struggle to put their internal experiences into words. Often in the early stages of working together, when I ask a client, "What are you sensing inside?" they respond with something like, "I learned to hide when my dad came home." When asked how they feel, many people respond with a thought, a story, or a description of a behavior, rather than a description of a feeling. But with time and practice comes more facility in naming internal experiences, and the answers might sound like, "I am noticing my energy pulling inward toward my belly, and the muscles in my thighs are tensing. I feel scared, like I want to hide."

Your body speaks an unambiguous language. It delivers valuable information that you have most likely learned to ignore. Other than fundamental somatic signals like hunger, thirst, elimination, and sexual desire, many folks are disconnected from their felt senses (and plenty of people are disconnected from these fundamental signals as well). They are far from being able to assess what they need accurately. They just can't feel it.

Perhaps you learned early that to feel was to be flooded and over-whelmed. Maybe you were told your feelings were too much, and maybe you were punished for them. You were told to stop crying. You were told you were okay when you weren't. Know that the reasons why you stopped feeling and stopped paying attention to your inner world are valid ones. Little you was doing the best you could.

The journey to the depths of your body is rigorous. I won't lie to you: you will have many things to feel and process on your path of deep somatic self-awareness, some of which might be uncomfortable. But you get to do it at your own pace, in small embodiment steps. You don't have to tackle the toughest parts yet, nor would I recommend it. Step by step, you will learn to live inside your body, opening up the potential for a lot of joy, power, and the true heart of your leadership to emerge.

While becoming an embodied leader takes time and energy, I believe it is indeed worth it. Becoming a leader who can feel yourself means you're tuning in to what matters to you. From the inside out, you learn to align your actions and practices with what feels right. A somatically aware leader can steer their organization with head and heart.

Chapter 1 Takeaways

- O Your body consists of three parts: your physicality, the stories you believe, and your practices.

- O You create your mindset, and you can question it by asking what you "should" do and be.

- O Your body speaks the language of sensation and emotion.

- O Muscle contractions are a way your body tries to keep you feeling safe and not overwhelmed.

2

LIVING IN YOUR BODY

THAT SUNDAY DAWNED like most others. I got out of bed and had coffee, planning how I would spend the sunny, warm January day. I had no idea that information from my body would turn my whole life upside down in a few short hours. There were no prophetic dreams, no flashing warning signs screaming "Major Life Pivot Ahead!" I was utterly clueless that my entire career would be on its head by the time the sun set, my company shuttered, and my future teetering on the brink. But that's precisely what happened.

I'd been building my company for three years. We had a brilliant team of six visionary, ultratalented folks on fire with the purpose of bringing relationship wellness to the masses. We were no stranger to the usual start-up roller coaster: founder's blues, running out of cash, and all the minutiae that are the weird world of starting a company. So what caused it all to come to a screeching halt that day? My body did! But before I tell you more, let's talk about embodiment and why it matters.

What Is Embodiment?

Embodiment is feeling yourself and feeling aware of the aliveness happening inside you—the aliveness of which you are a part, as a creature living in the world. Embodiment means really living inside your skin. Instead of being a brain on legs, you feel the fullness of your entire form. You both feel yourself in there *and* you are aware of feeling yourself in there.

Your attention plays a significant role in embodiment. When you are embodied, you place your attention on what is happening inside. When your brain is aware of your body in this way, it creates a level of mindful presence.

On a more expansive level, embodiment is when something has a physical form; it is tangible and corporeal. Embodiment can also mean a fullness of form, or the grounded and settled presence within a physical form. When something is embodied, it has a three-dimensional quality, with length, width, and depth.

To be embodied means you are the opposite of an empty shell. You live inside your body rather than outside it. You can place your attention inside you and hold it there. Embodiment is the integration of body and mind. When you are embodied, you feel yourself.

For the purposes of our work, I want to unpack the concept of "feelings." *Feelings* is an umbrella term that is used to describe both emotions and sensations. For the purpose of our work, it is helpful to be able to talk about emotions and sensations separately.

You experience emotions moving through your body. These are experiences of sadness, anger, joy, excitement, fear, grief, and so on. Emotions can move through your body quite quickly, if they aren't linked to a narrative. Buddhist author and teacher Pema Chödrön says it takes about ninety seconds for an emotional neurochemical response to complete. However, emotions can last for much longer when we feed them thoughts that sustain them.

Sensation, on the other hand, is all about the physical experiences in your body. Hunger, pain, pleasure, and thirst are all examples of sensation. But there is much nuance to sensation: for example, you might describe your body as feeling tight, full, contracted in your throat, hotness in your cheeks, energy in your legs, and the like.

Living and feeling inside your body is helpful to you as a leader in a myriad of ways. Intuition is a big one. You need to be able to feel and trust your instincts. With intuition, you can feel when things are correct, and you sense when something is off, either with an employee or a project. This is not magic. Your body perceives all kinds of information your mind is not consciously aware of. The key is being tuned in enough to listen.

For example, a few weeks before one of my employees quit in a blistering emotional outburst, my Spidey sense told me something was up. But I ignored this intuition because there were no outward signs of trouble. There had been no red flags or issues. But my gut told me, and after the employee left, I wished I had listened to what my body had been saying.

Somatic awareness is a profound way of knowing yourself. But where to start? The first step is to develop an awareness of what's happening inside you. This is mindfulness that includes your body. One way to achieve this is through mindfulness practices like meditation. There are many forms of meditation, ranging from those found in various spiritual traditions to secular, science-based methods. At their core, they are all ways of working with your attention. It takes time and repetition to learn to place your attention where you want it to be and to hold it there for any length of time. Remember how I mentioned that your brain is incredibly flexible? Mindfulness and meditation are powerful ways to tap into that flexibility and create new neural pathways, essentially training your brain to think differently.

But how do we apply this to our somatic work? How can we place attention in our tissues, in our muscles, if this is something we don't know how to do?

Here's the thing. When you were born, your embodiment was exquisite. You felt your feelings and noticed your sensations. When you had to pee, you just did it. When you were hungry, you cried until someone fed you. You kicked your tiny legs and wriggled your arms, and you felt every movement, every moment.

Over time, you directed your attention to other things. Schoolwork and learning, activities and relationships. You learned that feeling sometimes meant feeling too much. There were probably moments in your life when you wished your stomach would shut up, because you were too busy to eat. Or you didn't want to stop to stretch your cramped legs or go pee. You were told what you were feeling was wrong; for example, "It's not time to go to the bathroom right now," or "Sit still." And later, when you entered the world of work, you may have learned that focusing on your feelings got in the way of being productive.

The good news is that becoming embodied is about remembering. You had embodiment once, and you can have it again. All the reasons you moved your attention away from noticing your feelings and sensations were, at the time, good ones. You adapted to your environment. If you are now awakening to the awareness that you have been living a life of numbness, be gentle with yourself. You forgot about embodiment for good reasons.

In this chapter, you'll learn new ways to place your attention on your inner experience. You'll learn new ways to talk about your experience. All of this contributes to you being someone who lives in your skin.

Capacity and Overwhelm

When speaking of embodiment, we're talking about your capacity to feel and notice. I want you to be someone who can savor all your feelings and sensations. I want you to be a whole person everywhere in your life, and especially at work.

One thing that can prevent feeling is overwhelm. Overwhelm is when your system receives too much information at once. It is the feeling of "too much" or "I can't." It occurs when you're under stress, when there's too much to do, not enough time, or too much pressure. You can call this flooding your nervous system. Too much information to process. Too much fear, too much confusion. Too many tasks on your to-do list. It is not usually a pleasant experience for most people.

Each person's capacity is different. Your capacity is what you can manage at that moment, and it shifts depending on what's going on in your life. You have varying capacities, depending on how resourced you feel. An event that feels insignificant when you're well resourced can overwhelm you when you're not. We all have limits to what we can bear without feeling overwhelmed.

This is all a part of being human. Part of being an embodied leader is acknowledging the entirety of your humanity, and this includes acknowledging your capacity. I'll say it in different words: You *get* to have limits on your capacity. You get to decide what you can bear at any given time. Accepting and honoring this part of your humanity will help you recognize the humanity of others—including those you lead.

You have likely succeeded because you have a high capacity for handling complexity. When others need to stop and rest, you have developed strategies of perseverance and grit that enable you to continue. These are admirable qualities in a leader. However, every strategy has both costs and benefits. Your tenacity is likely rooted in your ability to do one or all of the following:

- ignore your needs
- push through your boundaries
- dig in and endure
- dissociate like a champ

Again, I want to emphasize that you learned these strategies as survival techniques. They were helpful to you, and they can definitely be useful in certain situations. But relying on them too much is a surefire path to overwhelm, as you have already likely experienced.

The Competencies You Need as a Leader

Leadership requires you to use many different muscles. You train and develop each one. As you practice, your muscles (competencies of leadership) grow. Naturally, some muscles may not be as strong as others, so you train the ones you most need to build.

You can train each of these skills through deliberate practice. Your skills live in your body; when you strengthen them, you strengthen your body as a leader. The capacities you want to develop tell you what you need to practice.

In my work as a business founder and boss, and as a coach to countless others over the years, I have found that leaders need the capacity to do the following:

- be present
- collaborate

- listen
- repair conflict
- trust and be trusted
- observe and name what is
- be curious
- envision
- inspire
- discern aligned action
- set boundaries
- decide
- take action
- receive support
- be with discomfort

PRACTICE MOMENT: Which Competencies Do You Want to Strengthen?

Grab your writing device.

As you read the list of leadership competencies above, mark a plus next to those you believe you already possess.

Now go back through the list and put a check mark next to the capacities you believe those you manage would say you possess.

Then write down the answers to these questions:

What leadership muscles do I need to cultivate?

What leadership muscles would my employees say I need to cultivate?

Go back to your list of new narratives you wish to embody. Where does a competency you want to acquire overlap with a new narrative you want to adopt? That place is fertile ground for change!

For now, just hold on to the narratives and competencies you long for. You don't need to do anything except let them be in your awareness. I'll walk you through the process of how to create somatic change in just a bit.

What Happens as You Become More Embodied

Fair warning: as you learn to focus on what's happening inside, you will notice more of your needs. If you could get by on five hours of sleep before, you may find that you need to pay attention to sleeping more. If you used to be able to skip breakfast and lunch, you will probably need more snacks as your body starts talking.

Becoming embodied means starting to listen to your body, which is essential for building trust with your body. This will enable you to have more compassion for the experiences and needs of others. In addition, your employees will trust your decisions more because they observe your groundedness and self-care. A well-rested, well-fed, hydrated boss who moves their body is more resilient, more patient, and more in tune with others.

The skills that got you into leadership are not necessarily the same skills that make you an excellent leader. In order to get where you are, you have likely had to hustle and grind, stay focused and exert effort. And it may be surprising to learn that hustling and grinding are not necessary skills for embodied leadership. Embodied leaders are not urgent. They are present. Your nervous system is guiding everyone you lead. Take note: *they will respond to how you are more than to what you say.*

In order to level up as a leader, you have to learn to *be* and to *feel* in a new way. It's a hard sell; I get it. Any hesitation or misgivings you're having as you read this are to be expected. You're being invited into new ways of thinking and being, and the old ways can get kind of testy about that. As you instigate a process of somatic change, you can be kind to the parts of you and the strategies that have gotten you where you are. Consider expressing gratitude to them and reassuring them you will call on them if needed.

As you age, this trusted body relationship becomes more and more valuable because it involves learning to prioritize long-term self-care over short-term gain. Remember that your body is your only friend who is there from your first breath until your last. It is an underutilized resource you have access to, for free, all the time. Want to know if someone's telling the truth? Do a gut check. Want to know what your next career move should be? Learn how to drop in and listen to the unequivocal truth your body offers. Your body doesn't speak in words. It speaks in feelings and sensation. Learning how to interpret this language is your new task.

While practice is at the core of becoming an embodied leader, there are a few principles to learn that will give you a solid foundation as you embark on your transformative journey.

Make an intention for attention. Your decision to become embodied guides your somatic learning journey. The deliberate placement of your attention helps you focus on what you're learning. By setting a course for somatic awareness, you will pay more attention to your felt sense. Returning to your intention is also helpful when the going is rough. Setting your intention is not something you do once and then forget about it. As a somatic learner, you set an intention every day to feel yourself more.

Your biological needs matter—and they might get loud! Here's a funny detail: when you practice embodiment, you'll probably notice you have to pee more. You may be thirstier, more tired, hungrier. You may want to move and stretch more than usual. All this is normal. Your body was always sending those signals, but now you're receiving them. I recommend that you act on them and give your body what it's asking for. This is a great way to build more trust with your body.

Your emotions are going to feel stronger. On this journey, you are bound to feel more emotions and to feel them more intensely. This is especially true at the beginning of somatic practice. If you are someone who has stayed safe by stuffing feelings down, it's okay—you're not alone. If you're worried that you'll be flooded with emotion to the point that you can't handle it, that's where a well-trained and supportive somatic coach can come in. It is possible to feel little by little, and you may want to find someone who can help you manage the flow without bursting the dam. You don't need to jump right into the deep end, and that's usually not the kindest thing you can do anyway. But if you're already here, welcome! The water's fine.

Your sensations will feel more substantial. As you reinhabit your body's organs and tissues, what you feel becomes more nuanced. For example, you will start to notice the chronic muscle contractions you use as a way to protect against overwhelm.

Attention is the currency of embodiment. Attending to your felt sense is how you become someone who lives inside yourself. Working with your attention gives you access to the benefits embodiment offers. Attention is the currency of any thriving relationship, including your relationship to your body. What you attend to grows and, ultimately, thrives.

PRACTICE MOMENT: Placing Attention

Find a comfortable place where you can sit uninterrupted for a few minutes and rest your hands gently on your lap. Now imagine placing your complete attention into one of your hands; it doesn't matter which one. Close your eyes and spend at least thirty to sixty seconds just being aware of your hand.

Pour your awareness into your fingertips, your palm. Feel how the bones exist inside and how the skin covers your fingers. If you like, you can massage your hand with your mind! Mentally attend to the top and bottom of your hand, the palm and backside, and the area around your fingernails. Can you feel where your wrist meets your palm? Can you feel each knuckle?

Continue to pay attention to your hand for as long as you want.

What do you notice after this period of focused attention on your hand?

How does the hand you attended to feel different from your other hand?

Nothing has changed other than that you placed your attention on your hand.

Whatever you notice is entirely normal.

Do you see how the attention we give something changes our awareness of it and relationship to it?

What Happens When You Don't Listen to Your Body: Meet Stan

While not a leadership story per se, the following story exemplifies how being embodied (or not) affects every area of your life. Stan's story is relevant because as a leader practicing embodiment, you need to be rigorously honest with yourself about your inner experience.

My client Stan came to me because his relationship with his partner, Ren, was in trouble. Stan didn't want to leave Ren, but he was finding that he didn't want to have a physically intimate relationship with them. Earlier in their relationship, Stan had been able to push through his feelings and be intimate with Ren, but then he would feel shame, resentment, and anger. Recently, it had gotten harder to have sex at all, but he was still pushing himself to do it, with no clue why he was so miserable.

Stan described himself as living above himself, looking down on himself most of the time. He described watching himself make decisions that felt wrong and making them anyway. He had been experiencing this sense of being outside himself for as long as he could remember.

Stan had developed a strategy of enduring, which meant he would hunker down, grit his teeth, and bear whatever hardship he was experiencing. It meant he would not speak up for himself. He would push through his own boundaries for the sake of pleasing others. As a result, he did not have a trusting relationship with his body. He had ignored his body cues for years, but now his body was getting louder. Things had reached a breaking point. Every time he would try to be intimate, his body would become nauseous. He would push, and his body would push back. Stan had minimal capacity for feeling his feelings and would go to great lengths to avoid it. If he shared something sad in a session, his eyes would fill with tears, but he would deny he felt sad.

Stan was very successful in his work. He said work was the only place he could relax. However, you will not be surprised to learn that although Stan enjoyed work, he also struggled in relationships with his colleagues because he was unable to say no to their requests. He often felt deeply resentful, but he hid his feelings and complied. Stan was the same person at work that he was at home.

My assessment was that Stan needed to learn to listen to his body and rebuild trust with himself. He needed to feel, but we had to go very slow. He became overwhelmed quite quickly. Feeling anything was terrifying for him. So our work started with having him place his attention on his big toe. He would look at his toe, wiggle it, and try to feel it. At each session, Stan practiced feeling more of himself: his feet. His hands. His chest. Slowly, he was able to stay present as he felt his whole self. It was progress, and we celebrated each new sensation he could handle.

Once Stan could feel himself, he couldn't force himself to have sex anymore. He had dissociated for a long time, and now he couldn't. Somatic awareness made it impossible to ignore what his body was telling him. So then our focus shifted to being able to talk more honestly with his partner about what he was feeling. Stan had to learn a whole new language around emotion. He had to learn to connect the sensations he felt with his emotions.

At that point, we'd been working together for about a year. Stan and Ren were not having sex, but they had not had an honest conversation about why. Ren knew Stan was doing this work with me but was not involved in it. Stan was starting to take baby steps to let his partner know how he felt, and we were both feeling optimistic.

But then he ran into a huge problem that threatened all the work we had been doing. Stan's partner had had enough. Because there had been no discussion, when sex stopped happening, Ren had taken it personally. They decided that Stan was having an affair. Ren was at the end of their capacity and said that unless things shifted dramatically, they would leave the relationship. Stan was devastated and felt he was entirely to blame.

Stan faced an immense challenge. Could he move forward quickly enough to save his partnership? And if he did, could he rebuild trust with Ren? He realized he had to tell Ren that for many years he had been having sex that he didn't want to have. He knew Ren would be hurt. Stan was in a catch-22. He couldn't go back to how it was before, because his body wouldn't let him. And to move forward, he would have to admit he had been lying.

When tears came into his eyes, he told me how sad and confused he felt. He was finally able to feel and name what he felt—but was it too late? We sat in a quiet moment together, and Stan's grief poured through him. He wasn't crying only for the situation with Ren, but for all he had lost as he had tried to stay safe from feeling. As Stan's flow of emotion slowed, I watched a shift come over his body. He looked like he was finally in himself, inhabiting his form. He was present and soft.

When he left my office that day, he decided that the cost of his old strategies was too great. He went home and told Ren everything. It was a conversation that lasted for hours, then days, then weeks. Now that the doors of communication were open, the two of them worked hard. With a lot of communication, they made it to the other side. Last I heard from Stan, they were doing great. He had continued his work of listening to and trusting his body, which had opened up the desire to start being intimate again, this time practicing verbal consent.

Like Stan, you have likely gotten to a point in your life when your old coping skills are causing more trouble than they're worth, when you are pushing yourself forward despite your body screaming at you to slow down and listen. And like Stan, you might experience growing pains when you start to pay attention to what your body's telling you, but in the end your courage and perseverance can lead to a deeper, more honest relationship to yourself and others. But first, you've got to feel yourself.

What Is Your Felt Sense?

In elementary school, you probably learned about the five senses: hearing, taste, sight, touch, and smell. But the truth is that your body receives information in far more than five ways! You have a lot of other cool senses that help you live your best life. You have sensory systems that provide information about balance (the vestibular sense), body position and movement (proprioception and kinesthesia), pain (nociception), and temperature (thermoception).

You feel hunger, fullness, thirst, itching, pain, pleasure, body temperature, nausea, tickling, the need to eliminate, physical exertion, tiredness, and sexual arousal, just to name a few. This information comes from within, from your felt sense. Another word for this felt sense is interoception. An important thing to note is that this is a physical experience, not a mental one. All of your sensory systems are constantly working, together and separately, and sending you information.

Although it's not talked about a lot, interoception—your felt sense—is a supremely important sense. It allows you to know what's going on with you. Your interoception is working all the time, monitoring all parts of your body, including your stomach, bladder, skin, muscles, and lungs. It sends information to your brain about how those body parts are feeling. How's your stomach right now? Are you hungry? Do you feel full? Bloated? Something else?

Your felt sense helps you know at every moment how you are feeling.

PRACTICE MOMENT: Explore Your Felt Sense

This is a great practice any time you want to quickly reconnect with yourself.

Take time and notice right now:

- What are you feeling?
- Where is your body in space?
- Is any part of your body moving?
- Do you need to pee?
- What's happening in your digestion?
- Are you thirsty?
- Can you feel your heartbeat?
- How is your body in contact with the chair, the ground?
- Where do you experience tightness, pressure, expansion, or temperature?

If you took a moment to answer the questions above, you accessed your felt sense. You accessed important information in your animal body. One way of thinking about felt sense is that it's about feeling into your aliveness. All living organisms share several processes of aliveness, including sensing, responding, regulating, developing, and processing energy. You have the power to notice the processes of life that are happening inside of you at any given moment. Your felt sense goes beyond your emotions. It is a tool of embodiment and can be accessed any time you feel the need to connect to yourself.

Naming What Is

A capacity you want to develop as an embodied leader is making accurate assessments and stating them. A critical somatic practice is *naming what is.* This starts with naming what is happening inside you. You can then become more adept at pinpointing what is happening outside of you. When you name what is, you describe, in the most precise terms possible, what you notice. Most of us have a relatively limited vocabulary for naming the sensations we experience. Becoming embodied means sensing greater nuance and documenting what you perceive in more detail. When Stan finally told Ren the truth, he named what is.

Because sensation and emotion are your body's languages, you need to expand your vocabulary. To interpret the information you're receiving, you need to translate sensation and emotion into words your brain understands. To start building your vocabulary, you can consult the list of feelings provided online by the Center for Nonviolent Communication (see the URL listed in the "Resources" section provided at the end of this book).

For example, one day you are on a hike. You are in a new forest, and a path captures your attention. You take a few steps and get a tingling sensation on the back of your neck. What does this mean? This is a fairly obvious example of trepidation. Your body is picking up danger cues. If you misinterpret them and continue down the trail, what might happen?

If you are about to go into a team meeting and feel a twisting, warm sensation in your stomach, what does that mean?

Name what is. Name the sensation. You can do this aloud or in your head: "I notice I feel a twisting, warm sensation in my stomach." When you name your experience, it gives you a moment to pause and consider: "Am I nervous about this meeting?" You can then ask yourself what you need: "What do I need before going to this meeting?"

Perhaps an employee says something that sounds fine during the meeting, but you notice your shoulders tighten. You suddenly feel jittery. Name it in your head: "I feel my shoulders tense. I am feeling jittery." Naming what is gives you a moment to notice. To feel. To observe. To slow down. Then you can ask yourself, "What about their comment feels off? What am I picking up on?" Tuning into your felt sense in this way can help you access your body's wisdom so you may more fully assess what is happening in the moment, both inside and outside you.

PRACTICE MOMENT: Name What Is

What is, right now? Name it. The following is a simple three-step practice for naming what is inside you. This is an essential somatic tool that you can access regularly throughout your day.

1. Observe your body, and choose an area of it that is talking to you.

2. Notice the sensations. Which words name what you feel? Try to find three to five descriptive words or phrases.

3. Hang out in that place for as long as it's interesting. What happens? Does the sensation shift? Does it stay the same? How would you name it now?

Embodiment vs. Body Awareness

Many practices require body awareness, but they are not, by default, embodiment practices. Any athlete, dancer, or person doing physical labor has body awareness. Embodiment is different in that it requires conscious placement of attention on your *inner* experience. With intention, you place your attention on your emotions and sensations.

Embodiment includes:

• learning how to place your awareness inside your body

• remembering to seek wisdom from your body

• listening to and paying attention to your physical, emotional, spiritual, and relational needs

• being aware of your emotions

• developing your internal felt sense

Embodied Role Models

Something that can be incredibly helpful in any growth journey is finding a role model who you feel exemplifies the qualities you want to develop. I encourage you to give some thought to whom you might choose as your embodiment role model. Some things to consider:

- Whom do you know who has access to their body wisdom?
- Who lives inside of their experience?
- Who trusts their gut?
- Who gives themselves permission for enough rest, movement, hydration, and nourishment?
- Who in your life is present?
- Who tends to their own care?

You may or may not have a role model come to mind. Or you may have an anti-role model, someone who is *not* embodied in the ways you wish to be. That person can be equally instructive. As examples, I'll share the story of my anti-embodiment role model, and then I will introduce you to the person from whom I learned to be embodied.

During one winter, I lived with a professional ballerina. She worked her body eight to ten hours a day, seven days a week, every week. She lived on grapefruit, air-popped popcorn, and miso soup. She told me she was one of the few ballerinas who did not smoke like a chimney and did not have an eating disorder. She was certain she was on the healthy side of things.

But every night, I would watch her gulp ibuprofen by the handful and apply ice to her misshapen toes and calves. She was in chronic, self-induced pain. Here was a young woman who had utterly dedicated her life to her craft and made her living through her body. She was body aware, but she was not embodied. Needless to say, while I admired her talent and dedication to her art, she was not my embodied role model.

Much later in life, I met Meredith, the person who would become my somatics mentor, teacher, and coach, and my embodied role model. Every week for years, I would go to her office, and we would practice feeling together, emotions and sensations. Her leadership depended on feeling herself and naming what she was feeling.

She tracked my body closely. She noticed when I breathed deeply and when I stopped breathing. She saw when my attention needed to flee the room and gaze out at the hills of San Francisco. She noticed when I came back. She saw these things, and when appropriate, she gently drew my attention to them. With her help, I learned to notice and then to regulate my nervous system.

"How's your mood?" she would ask, or "How's the breathing going?" With my coach's guidance, I was able to find my way back to remembering that I had a body. I relearned feelings, sensations, and needs happening inside. Through this work, I learned not to dismiss my humanity and not to let anyone else ignore it.

My somatic coach's embodiment means she has access to herself. She can feel what is true for her. She has developed the skill of naming her experience in a way that is helpful to others. She can name what is.

For now, consider whom you might want as a role model. Someone who trusts themselves and their experience. Someone who has integrity and dignity. Someone who takes up the amount of space they need.

Chapter 2 Takeaways

○ Embodiment happens when you feel yourself and name your sensations and emotions.

○ Sensations are internal movements, tensions, temperatures, expansions, pains, and pleasures.

○ Emotions are feelings like sadness, joy, and grief.

○ Embodiment is a choice. You choose it with your attention.

○ Who you are at home is who you are at work, and vice versa. You take your body everywhere with you.

3

MUSCLE CONTRACTIONS

INSIDE OF YOU, you have habitual ways of holding and tensing your muscles. These habits were born from an impulse to manage your internal experience. You learned at an early age that bracing or tightening could help you survive difficult situations. This impulse comes from instincts humans developed over the course of evolution to respond to threats in the wild. They are a sign that your body wants to work to help you. The key is learning to communicate with your body so it works *with* you.

Muscular contractions are essential information. When you contract your muscles, you are trying to cope with your feelings. It's like putting on armor. Wilhelm Reich, one of the founders of modern psychoanalysis, talked about armoring as chronic muscle contraction that occurs in horizontal bands across your body. These bands include your eyes, jaw, throat, pectoral muscles and heart, shoulders, abdominals, and pelvic floor.

People sometimes experience contractions as feeling blocked. I hear clients say things like, "I feel blocked around my heart," or "I can't access my gut." Have you ever felt blocked around something in your work or personal life? Chances are there's a physical correspondence. Muscular contractions and energetic blocks go together like cream in coffee. If you're tightening some part of yourself, your life energy can't flow through that part.

Contractions can be physical, energetic, emotional, or mental. We get contracted around situations, people, and decisions. Contractions are both a blessing and a burden. They are a blessing because they shine the light on exactly where your attention is needed. They are a burden because they can keep you stuck, often in pain. It's helpful to learn to work with them in a gentle manner. As you learned in chapter 1, somatic change is a process. Choice follows awareness. So you must first become aware of your contractions and blocks before you can choose to work with them.

Remember, your body is wise. The point of becoming aware of your muscle contractions is not to relax them, at least not initially. Any muscle contraction offers you a way to understand yourself more deeply. Eventually, that information will be the gold of your leadership. When you have done the work to understand how your body responds somatically to stress, you'll quickly notice when something feels off, and you'll be able to address it. Leaders who can feel themselves can respond to the information bodies share. Wouldn't it be helpful if that clenching in your jaw could help you know that the candidate sitting across from you in the interview isn't the right one?

Becoming Aware of Contractions

As you become somatically aware, you'll become aware of your habituated contractions. This is a point where some people get frustrated. After all, you're becoming embodied to feel better, not to feel more discomfort! But first you have to feel what is. Then you get more choice.

As your attention shifts more and more toward your body, you will become aware of exactly where you are contracted. For example, if you do a quick body scan right now, what part feels tight? Your neck? Shoulders? Gut? Butthole? You often develop chronic pain at places where you habitually contract your muscles. This pain can help you become aware of your contractions.

Muscle contraction can cause an impact on the tissues around the muscle, including nerve impingement. It is not uncommon to feel emotionally numb, often with a corresponding physical numbness.

When I became somatically aware, I realized that I habitually held my left shoulder tight toward my ear. I was confident that teaching that part of my body to relax was the thing to do. If only that shoulder would stay down, I would feel easy and free! But no matter how many times I forced it to relax, back upward it would creep. It restricted my breathing, and it created pain and tightness in my neck that caused chronic headaches.

I felt frustrated by my lack of progress, convinced that my shoulder held the key to my healing. Instead of forcing my shoulder to relax, my somatic coach encouraged me to have my partner hold it each night. Every night I would lie on my side, and my partner would pull my shoulder into the contracted position that it gravitated toward. In essence, he was taking over the contraction. He would hold the shoulder in that position while the muscles inside learned to release. We did this nightly for a year. I had to retrain my muscles to work differently.

Around this time, I started lifting heavy weights at the gym. I worked with a trainer who pushed me hard. When I would bench press or do anything intense with my pectoral muscles, I would start to cry. I was embarrassed and confused by this, and I would walk around the gym until it passed.

The strange part was that I had no story about what was happening. It was all sensation. Using my muscles in new ways meant that the numbness from the chronic shoulder tension was leaving my body. I understood on a deep level—not just in my mind—that this contraction had helped me cope with overwhelming situations. Trauma had been stored in my tissues. Now that I was moving in new ways, trauma was being released. Although I had experienced much Western psychoanalysis focused on treating trauma with talk therapy, I was now learning how important somatic work—independent of the trauma story—was for my healing.

Now, years later, that contraction in my shoulder is not typically present. It does happen from time to time. When it does, I know it's sending me the message that something doesn't feel safe, or something feels like too much. I know I'm feeling a need to protect myself. That contraction is pure gold, like an early warning system!

This leads to an essential somatic truth.

Support the Contraction

A special type of magic happens when you allow what is already happening in your body to happen. This is the transformative quality of somatics. You trust the wisdom of your body, so instead of fighting against what is, you permit it. You offer it support and care and kindness. When you support the contraction, you let it be what it is. You let it do what it does.

For example, let's say your hips are really tight. You do squats, yoga, hip openers, and they are still tight. You've done everything you can to get your hips to relax, but it's not happening. There is one important thing to try: support your tight hips. Let them be tight. Lie on the floor with a mountain of pillows. Ask a trusted loved one to press your hips into the floor. Or you can compress them with a belt, cinching it tight to help hold the contraction in place.

Your body is wise, and it's doing its best to keep you safe. So let it.

If you are someone who curls in around your midline and are constantly trying to remember to pull your shoulders back and open your chest, try an experiment of allowing your body to do what it wants to do. Follow it.

This may sound illogical to you, even absurd. When my somatic coach first told me about the concept of supporting the contraction, it felt scary, dangerous, and misinformed. I thought that if I just allowed my shoulder to do what it wanted to do, I'd be done for. If I offered it love and permission, it would not only continue to do what it did; it would get even more intense! Why would I want to be kind to something that was hurting me? Here I was trying to stop the contraction from happening, which I considered to be the only logical response, but my somatic coach was telling me to support it instead. It didn't make any sense, and I was wary. But I did what she said—and my shoulder shifted. Not only did my shoulder contraction shift, but how I was in the world started to feel easier. I had access to more of myself. I felt freer.

When you support something that is already happening, you send the message, "It's okay, I trust you." But don't worry; the contraction won't be like that forever. You won't be permanently curled inward or pressed into the floor until you die. When you allow what is happening to happen, things shift of their own accord. You don't have to force yourself to relax.

After the experience with my shoulder, I realized how supporting the contraction was helpful. This is true in situations both somatic and otherwise. Instead of getting into a fight with reality, this is a secret strategy that brings greater ease.

For example, I worked with a client named Mike who was struggling to feel generous with everyone in his life, including his family, his brother, and his employees. Sitting in my office, Mike said several times, "I am so selfish." It was clear there was a lot of emotion behind those words. I asked Mike to support the contraction by asking him to let himself be selfish, just for right now, and see what happened. Initially, he was concerned that allowing himself to feel the selfish part would ramp it up. But because he trusted our work, he said it again, and this time, a wail emerged from his throat. He grieved, crying, for several minutes.

Once he stopped crying he told me how his older brother had always told him how selfish he was when they were kids. Recently, his brother had been diagnosed with ALS, and Mike longed to feel closer to his brother and to be able to support him and his family. But every time he tried to do something to support his brother, Mike felt conflicted. Part of him wanted to, and part of him wanted to spend his time doing something more fun. He felt very judgmental of himself and was now labeling himself with the label his brother had used all those years ago.

Once Mike was in touch with his grief, he realized that the grief was about longing to feel connected with his brother, and how scared he was about his brother's illness. Supporting the contraction allowed Mike to open to the feelings that had been blocked, and he could determine a path forward with his brother that felt aligned with the present instead of the past.

Most people become concerned when they first hear the suggestion to support the contraction. They worry, as I did, that allowing it to happen will empower it to get stronger and stronger. It makes sense that we would think this way. We have probably been told repeatedly throughout our lives not to feel what we are feeling, to suck it up, to get over it. But with contractions, and with feelings in general, trying to force them to relax or go away doesn't work. When you give them something to fight, they will keep on fighting back. So why not try something else? Supporting the contraction allows it to move and release. Not only that: until you support it, it will persist.

The contraction is there to give you insight. It is a library of you. Therefore, the way to be with a block or a contraction is to gently move your attention toward it. You don't try to shift it, change it, fix it, or figure it out. You allow your body to lead the process. While holding that part of yourself, you can ask, "What does this part of my body need right now?" or "How does this part of my body want to move?" You may also try applying pressure or bringing loving attention to that area of your body. Perhaps you want to add temperature, such a hot-water bottle or a cool stone.

Supporting the contraction works for physical muscle contractions as well as for emotional blocks you're experiencing. In fact, the physical and the emotional are almost always connected. Unprocessed emotions like fear, grief, and anger can get somaticized. That means that unresolved feelings can become physical ailments. For example, every time Mike feels sad he pushes that emotion down into his belly and unconsciously holds it there by contracting the muscles in his abdomen. Eventually, a contraction like this can lead to the development of a physical illness.

If you're feeling blocked from your emotions, you can apply the principle of supporting the contraction. Move toward the absence of feeling. Tell yourself it's okay to not feel, and get curious about what exactly not feeling is like. Explore the space of not feeling, without making it wrong or bad that you are not feeling. Numbness or absence of sensation is deeply protective.

Any time you notice you're contracting, that's your body asking for more attention and support. As you begin to notice your contractions, you have the opportunity to become kinder to and more supportive of yourself.

PRACTICE MOMENT: Support the Contraction

Where do you feel contracted?

You may immediately notice a tightness in your body. Perhaps you feel something akin to congestion around the space of your heart, or maybe in your belly or genitals. Maybe it has been ages since you've cried, and you can feel the backlog of grief as if behind a wall in your chest.

One quick way to get in touch with contractions is to ask yourself what you wish was different. Do you wish your mother would finally understand you? Do you wish your partner would ask about your day before launching into theirs? Do you wish your neck wouldn't hurt? Do you wish your employee would turn in their reports without needing a reminder? What else do you wish were different?

As you think about something you wish were different, notice what happens in your body. Check your eyes, your jaw, your throat. Your chest. Your hands. Your butt. Check your breath. Notice if anything feels tight. Notice, too, if this feeling of tightness is familiar.

Another way to understand your contractions is to check in with the parts of your body where you usually hold tension. How's the back of your neck today? Your shoulders?

Now that you've identified some contractions in your body, let's test this principle.

Remember when you poured your attention and aliveness into your hand? Do this again, but for both hands this time. Bring the kindest, most loving parts of you forward and into your hands.

When you feel ready, place your love-filled hands on the contraction, and let them hang out there for a while. Don't try to change or fix anything. Be present with yourself for a minute or more, as long as you like, until this is not interesting anymore.

Then ask yourself:

- What do I notice?

- What happens when I support my contraction with gentleness?

Remember, supporting the contraction isn't the final step in the process. It's the first step in accepting what is. After you support the contraction, you will have more choices.

If you want to go deeper into this practice, get curious about whether your body wants to assume a shape or move in

any way right now. Follow your intuition, and then hang out in
that movement or shape until it feels complete. What happens
when you allow your body to do what it wants to do instead of
fighting against it?

Resisting Is Important!

What have you tried to learn that requires practice? A new skill or hobby?
A craft? Becoming a leader requires training. Becoming embodied involves
practice. Yet many people struggle with maintaining practice. Some resistance to taking up a new practice is normal and to be expected. Many of
us have been taught to believe that this resistance is some kind of personal
failure. But the intentions of resistance, like the intentions of contractions,
are good, and you can learn to work with resistance kindly. In fact, resistance is integral to change.

Our egos don't want to do things we are not already good at. We crave
the positive feedback loop of mastery. Once you've developed competence
in any area of your life, it can feel pretty challenging to become a beginner
again. Simply put, competence feels good, and not-yet-competent feels
pretty crappy.

If, as a child, you had to practice something you didn't want to practice
or study something you didn't want to study, you probably experienced
some resistance. Even though you are pushing yourself to practice now, I'm
guessing your rebellious inner teen isn't having it.

One reason resistance is there is to protect you from failing. It sends
you the message that if you don't try, you won't fail. Resistance is essentially
about front-loading failure. If you resist, you have responsibility for and
control of the outcome. It may not feel great, but at least you're in charge.
If you have ever tried to develop a new practice only to quit and feel that
you let yourself down, welcome to your resistant self.

Like all your protective parts, resistance is a strategy. It takes care of
your desire not to fail. Let's normalize any resistance you feel to becoming
more embodied. It's normal, it happens, and it's okay. Although resistance
may have stopped you before, and you may wish it would go away, you

now understand contraction. Resistance is just another type of contraction, which you now know how to work with.

Invite gentle, nonjudgmental curiosity about your resistance. One function of resistance is to protect you from failure. Another is to act like brakes for your system. Resistance can provide a helpful pause that allows space for discernment. If you feel resistant to a specific practice, it could be your fear talking. But it could also be that this is not the proper practice for you or the right time in your life to begin it.

Resistance invites you into deeper knowing of yourself, if you let it. It welcomes your curiosity, wisdom, and power of discernment. When you feel your resistance talking to you, you can ask it questions. When you inquire with gentleness and listen to your responses, you build self-trust.

Gentle inquiry sounds like:

- What am I resisting?
- What is my resistance taking care of?
- Am I feeling scared of something?
- Is this the right practice for me?
- Is this the right time in my life for this practice?

It can be helpful to reflect on things you have quit over the course of your life. Which things did you quit because you were resistant? How do you feel now about quitting that particular thing? Do you notice any patterns to your resistance? And are there any times when resistance was a true friend to you? Has resistance helped keep you safe or helped you admit an uncomfortable truth?

For example, my partner and I decided to train in aikido several years ago. It was the first time either of us had ever practiced martial arts. It was hard as hell, fun, painful, and hard as hell some more. After about a year and a half, we both quit going to our dojo without discussing why. In retrospect, I realize we were overwhelmed with the intensity of the practice. Recently, when we were cleaning out closets, my partner found his *gi*, the garment you wear when you train. He shoved it into the donation bag without a second thought.

My *gi* was still hanging in my closet, and I couldn't bear to part with it. I felt sad about leaving training. I felt that my resistance had gotten the better of me. I hoped to be able to return someday, and hanging onto the *gi* meant that door wasn't closed forever.

This became an opportunity for us to talk about it. I found that my partner didn't feel sad or guilty about quitting aikido at all! He didn't feel as if he had failed. He felt like he had wanted to do it, he did it, and he found it wasn't quite the right practice for him. He enjoys weight training and dancing more than aikido. For him, resistance helped him recognize that he wasn't in the right practice. Not every practice that you pick up and try on will fit; and of those that do, they won't all fit forever.

My somatic coach always says she is committed to permanent practice, but she is not committed to a *particular* permanent practice. She is committed to being someone who practices with intention. Your practices will shift and change as your needs do. You may stick with some practices for the rest of your life. There may also be some practices that are appropriate for a certain amount of time, and then it's okay to say goodbye.

Resistance can illuminate our fears, perhaps showing us places where we want to lean in and say yes to the challenge. But resistance can also be a superpower, showing us where we need to set boundaries. When you resist, you say no. You say no *clearly*. When you resist yourself, it can suck, but it can also mean facing the truth. Resistance can lead you to discerning deeper ways you can intentionally take care of yourself.

Ask yourself: what is the most awesome and helpful thing you resist?

Shifting the Shape of You

While contractions are initially well intentioned, they're also bossy. They determine the way you feel in your body. When you have habituated muscle contractions, your freedom and choice are limited. Contractions may offer protection, but it comes at a steep cost.

The costs of contraction include:

- lack of feeling and sensation
- lack of access to the wisdom that part of your body holds
- increased chance of injury or disease
- chronic tightness or pain

- lack of access to feeling what the contractions are masking
- lack of freedom to release contractions as you wish

Think again of that cypress tree on the Northern California coast. When the tree was young, its branches were flexible. They moved easily in the wind, returning to a neutral position when the wind ceased. They responded and adjusted to their environment. But as the tree aged and thickened, that shape became immutable. The branches are now constantly bowed in one direction. There is no flexibility, no ability to respond to the wind if by chance it started blowing from the opposite direction. The woody structure of that tree has determined the shape in which it will live out its life.

Your contractions have a similar strategy. If left unaddressed, they will determine how you live your life. They will decide the shape of you. Your contractions can cause you to become rigid and unmoving in your actions and thinking. This is opposite to the sensual aliveness that embodiment and choice invite you into.

As an embodied leader, you need the freedom to respond to your environment. You need to be able to choose how you react to situations as they arise. Investigating your habituated contractions gives you an opportunity for more flexibility and liberty. Once you move beyond your habits, you get to explore the question, "What else is possible for me?"

That's when your tissues become more pliant. Your range of motion increases in both your physical and emotional realms. You develop more capacity to be with complexity.

As you reinhabit your form, you will feel more of *everything*. For instance, many of my clients have trauma that causes them not to feel parts of their bodies. As they regain access to their felt sense of those parts, it is not unusual for them to begin experiencing any of the following sensations, in any order:

- numbness
- tingling
- pain
- prickling

- awareness of that part of the body all the time

- related pain or impact

It's important here to note that disembodiment happens as a response to trauma. Disembodiment is a result of chronic dissociation. Dissociation is one of the somatic strategies humans (and other animals) use to survive painful and threatening situations.

Early humans developed a fight-or-flight response to deal with threats and dangers. This is an automatic response to danger, and it allows you to react quickly, without the need to think. The amygdala is the part of your brain responsible for this reaction. When you feel stressed or afraid, the amygdala releases stress hormones that prepare your body to fight the threat or flee from the danger. This is a good and necessary thing.

The other somatic strategies for dealing with threat are appeasement, collapse, and dissociation. Dissociation is an adaptive response to threat and is a form of "freezing." It is employed as a strategy when fighting and fleeing are not feasible options.

Dissociation is what possums do. When faced with threat, their central nervous systems shut down and they involuntarily pass out. They freeze. They play dead. They wait for the danger to pass. This is an amazing strategy.

With dissociation, we simply move our attention from what is happening to somewhere else. Some people create a safe space deep inside. Some people move their attention outside their body. Dissociation is a very helpful survival tool.

Dissociation is not inherently a problem. The trouble starts when that strategy is the only one you have to ease your suffering. To be clear, most of us who dissociate are not consciously choosing to move our attention away from our bodies. It just becomes easier and easier over time. Many elements of Western culture support the practice, including substances that numb you and media that helps you to forget yourself.

Many people spend most of their time and attention not living inside their own skin. However, inside your body is where you can connect with your humanity. You can feel the impact you create. You can feel the impact you experience. Being embodied is how you can make really good, connected, whole-body decisions that honor the humanity of everyone, especially those you lead.

Because disembodiment results from trauma, and you are now learning to live an embodied life, please know that as you return your attention to your body, unexpected memories may arise, and there may be points when the work feels overwhelming. If this happens, remember that you can always dial back on the intensity. You can take a break. It is totally fine to move slowly, and in fact, it's more effective. I also highly recommend seeking professional support. In my opinion, the gold standard is somatics practitioners. Somatic Experiencing, EMDR, and other trauma-informed somatic modalities (see the list in the "Resources" section) have been proved effective in helping to process traumatic memories that live in the body. While it is outside the scope of the book to provide support for PTSD symptoms, if this is happening to you, you deserve care and support, and I encourage you to seek it out.

Developing Somatic Awareness through the Paradigm of Practice

We are what we practice.
And we are always practicing something.
—RICHARD STROZZI-HECKLER

A practice is anything at all that you do. I don't mean *practice* as in learning to play a musical instrument or meditation practice. Practices are the choices you make about how you allot your attention. The choices you make about what you practice can be conscious or unconscious. If you live your life without intention about what you practice, you are still practicing.

If you were forced to practice anything when you were young, this conception of what practice means is a reframe. You get to choose to practice what you want to have in your life. Centering your life around the things you want to practice puts you in the driver's seat.

Personal change happens through developing somatic awareness and learning to pay attention to your survival responses and the internal landscape of your body, including your subtle sensations and emotions. You learn to notice your embodied narratives. You begin to attend to your practices. You choose new narratives and then select new practices that support them.

Holding a practice paradigm for your life is how you can get the good stuff. For example, let's say you have a narrative that you are unlovable. You've been practicing that tired old bone for years and are ready to move on from it. Well, what are you going to practice instead? Maybe you decide that you want to feel lovable, so you figure out some practices for that.

A practice for the "I am lovable" narrative might involve taking a moment to try to feel it when someone says they love you. Or maybe you develop a practice of looking in the mirror and saying, "I love you."

Practices are not monolithic. Just because you start a practice, that doesn't mean you have to continue it forever. You do it until you get what you want or need out of it, and then stop if you want to. And then you can return to it later if you need to. You don't need to be rigid with yourself. You can commit to the practice paradigm rather than committing to a particular practice forever.

There is a sweet spot between being gentle with yourself and beating yourself up if you stop engaging in a practice you intend to do. Find practices that light you up, that you want to do. If you get resistant about a practice, stop and discern why before giving up on it. Do you need more support to do that practice? More structure? Transitions are pretty hard on routine practices, so know that in times of even small changes, you'll need to pay extra attention to your practices.

If you stop doing a practice and then feel shame and guilt about it—so much so that you feel like you failed—then what? Simple: tell someone. Then do the practice just once to assess whether it's still the proper practice, or if your resistance was telling you a truth you needed to hear. You will fall off of your practices at some point; when this happens, you can simply start again, or tweak the practice if needed. If it's time to say goodbye to a particular practice, acknowledge the ending, and find gratitude for what you've gained from that practice.

Here's another example of how it works. Let's say you want to be someone who can say about your life, "I am free." So you practice doing things that help you feel free. You travel. You eat what you want. You practice freedom, whatever that means to you. Your narratives are what you believe to be true about the world ("I am free"), and your practices support them (acting freely).

To continue the example, before you decided you wanted to be someone who feels free, perhaps you believed in the narrative "I am stuck." What were you practicing that made you feel stuck? What were the things you did or didn't do that supported that narrative of stuckness? Maybe you practiced not giving yourself permission. Maybe you practiced limiting your food. Maybe you followed a set routine without being open to new sources of joy. Whatever you practiced, it supported the "I am stuck" narrative.

Over the course of this book, you'll be trying on many new practices, and you'll see which ones stick. When you choose a practice, you're making a choice about how to allocate your time and attention. Finding the right practices for yourself is crucial. It's a process of getting curious and experimenting. Think about it as if you're dating that practice for a time-limited period, or conducting a series of interviews, during which you collect data about that practice's effects so you can decide if you're a good match. Ask yourself if you like it. Does the practice help you? Is it the right practice, or the right practice right now? Get curious about any contractions or resistance you feel. Ask your body what it is trying to tell you.

You'll probably find some of the new practices offered in this book helpful; others, not so much. You might even dislike a few! Take a discovery bite of each one. Try it on at least once. If you don't like it, you never have to do it again—unless your curiosity about why you hated it gets the better of you. Later in your journey, you may find that you've become ready for what it has to offer.

Finding your new right practices is the core of the change you're trying to make. To be an embodied leader, you have to do practices that support that narrative. What are your practices of embodied leadership?

Remember the story I began this chapter with, about closing my company? Now I'll tell you the rest of the story about how being an embodied boss helped me know when it was time to shut our doors. That fateful day in January, I received an email from an upset customer. There I was, trying to build a company offering relationship wellness, and a customer was angry with me. When I read that email, I understood that the customer was right, and I got angry with my company—and with myself. Then I felt a flash of shame pour through my body. The truth in my body was undeniable. I realized I had stepped out of my integrity to try to keep the company going.

After months of start-up woes, during which time I convinced myself I couldn't give up and had to keep pushing, the writing was finally on the wall—all because my body told me. Now, to be clear, this wasn't the first time I had thought of closing the company. We were struggling and had been holding on fiercely. The pandemic, the lack of access to capital as a minority founder, and the unpredictable revenue had all been piling up on top of all the regular start-up problems. I didn't read one email and then pull the plug. I'm not talking about being impulsive or not thinking things through. Ending the company had been on my mind for a long time, but I hadn't known how to make the decision.

So when that flash of shame propelled through my body, I knew something was wrong. Something wise and brave inside me said, "Nothing is worth feeling like this." I walked out of my living room into the kitchen and told my partner, "I'm done."

Those flashes of deep truth are rare. They're valuable. Because I practice being embodied every day, when it hit I knew what it was, and I listened. No boss ever wants to make that call, but sometimes you have to. Sometimes the right choices are the most difficult ones.

I'm grateful for the embodiment that allowed me to know and feel the truth in the right moment. I'm grateful that I can feel when I'm in integrity and when I'm not. Under duress, your body will do what it has practiced. When stressed, we return to what is familiar. Because I'd had a long somatic awareness practice, I was able to feel and name and take decisive action, based on wisdom arising from my body. My body *was* my leadership. This is what I mean when I say "developing the body of a leader." In the next chapter, you'll learn the foundational skills to do just that.

Chapter 3 Takeaways

O   Internal muscle contractions are one way you take care of yourself when things are overwhelming.

O   Contractions can be both physical and emotional. You notice them through resistance.

O   Supporting the contraction means just letting your body do what it is already doing.

O   Support the contraction first, even if you are scared that it will lead to more contraction.

O   Once the contraction has felt significantly permitted and allowed, something new will open up.

O   When you feel resistance to a practice, you can ask yourself if it's not the right practice or not the right time, or if there's something else inside you that needs tending.

4

FOUNDATIONAL EMBODIMENT SKILLS

IN THIS CHAPTER YOU'LL LEARN foundational somatic practices that support embodiment. You may already know some of these skills and practice them regularly, or this may be entirely new information. Somatic learning is not like book learning. In traditional learning, you study a topic and internalize the information. But somatic learning is lifelong learning: the nuances of sensation increase with time and practice, and you become adept at recognizing and naming your inner experience, but there is no point when you are "done" and can graduate.

As a somatic learner, you are committing to curiosity and exploration. When I say *curiosity*, I mean your interest in your own aliveness. Cultivating curiosity means becoming comfortable with not knowing. You get to be present and notice. One of my mentors says, "Be available for surprise." Curiosity is the foundation that embodiment is built on. Your internal state is always shifting and changing. The more embodied you become, the more you realize the fluidity of your aliveness.

Get to Know Your Nervous System

The main tools of somatic learning are intention and attention. You are deciding to practice and then noticing what you feel when you do. This is how you become empowered to operate your nervous system.

In many ways, humans are at the mercy of their nervous systems. You have no control over what messages get sent. The transference of electrical impulses from neuron to neuron is happening automatically, without your approval. You then react to the impulses sent via your nerves. Your belly sends hunger messages to your brain. Your brain responds by directing your attention toward food. These are primitive survival responses.

Let's delve into the neuroscience, just a bit, to get a basic understanding of how you work, according to the polyvagal theory developed by Stephen Porges.

Your autonomic nervous system is made of two main branches: sympathetic and parasympathetic. The sympathetic branch is in the middle part of your spinal cord. It helps you to act, and quickly. It tells your brain to release adrenaline, which triggers your fight-or-flight response. This is the upregulation mechanism of excitement, arousal, and heightened response. The sympathetic branch can be thought of as your aggressive defense system.

The parasympathetic branch of your nervous system contains your vagus nerve, which travels from your brain stem in two directions: downward to your heart, stomach, diaphragm, and lungs, and upward to connect with your eyes, neck, ears, and throat. This can be thought of as your social engagement system.

The vagus nerve is important because it supports feelings of safety as well as responses to danger. The ventral vagal pathway is the part of the vagus that helps you feel safe and connected. When the dorsal vagal pathway is activated, it removes those feelings of safety and connection, and instead you feel collapsed, frozen, or numb. Dissociation is a result of the response of the dorsal vagal pathway. This can be thought of as your passive defense system.

Knowing basic information about your nervous system helps you understand that when you're triggered, there are biological processes happening that are beyond your control. Your choice is found in working with your system instead of against it. Developing compassion for your experience is key.

Let's look at how knowing more about your nervous system can help you have a better quality of life. The pop psychology you hear about embodiment often consists of sentiments like, "Slow down. Take a deep breath." While many people find this technique helpful for returning to their bodies and grounding themselves, it is not a one-size-fits-all solution.

Pat Ogden, a wise and experienced teacher of somatics, talks about working with clients who breathe very shallowly. For these clients, a deep breath would not be helpful; it would be overwhelming. Slowing down and taking a deep breath is simply not within their current capacity. They have developed a survival strategy that relies on breathing shallowly. They need to be able to move quickly, ready to escape at any moment. For these clients, Pat recommends tiny "sips" of air. This helps as they learn to feel safe by bringing more air into their systems. Similarly, for trauma survivors, breathing deeply can be intensely triggering. Your nervous system is unique to you, and you can learn to operate it according to your specific needs.

Your nervous system affects all areas of your life. For example, many of my clients report feeling anxious. They describe the experience of anxiety as feeling buzzy, vibrating, jittery, and fearful. They talk about not being able to sit still, concentrate, or settle. It wouldn't be helpful for me to tell them to calm down. Instead, we meet their nervous systems where they are by practicing self-regulation through movement. I teach them strategies for feeling what's happening inside and then making a choice about how they want to work with it. Later in this chapter, I'll share some of those strategies with you.

All of this is to say: begin where you are. There is no perfect embodiment. You can develop embodiment at any point in your life. There is nothing you are striving toward other than knowing how you feel. There is nowhere to get to, no goal, except feeling the full extent of your sensations and emotions. For this, you must build capacity. You build the capacity to feel yourself, without judging how you feel. You build capacity to be with what is inside your experience.

In his book *Holding the Center,* Richard Strozzi-Heckler illustrates this principle when he writes: "If we are capable of experiencing our sensations it's possible to laugh, cry, yell, demand, desire, protest, accept, and love. If we anesthetize ourselves from feeling sensation, our emotional range will shrink and with it the capacity for effective action, passion for life, and the ability to sustain meaningful relationships."

The capacity for feeling is built slowly over time. You dip your attention into your body, as you might dip a toe into an unknown body of water to test the temperature. You notice how your system is doing. You remember to bring your attention back to your body below your neck. And then you uncover exciting information.

Humans are both reactive and responsive. By *reactive,* I mean acting quickly without thinking; by *responsive,* I mean taking the time to pause and discern the wise decision. We need the speed of our nervous system to react to immediate danger. If a building is burning, you want to get people out right away, rather than stopping to consider the best course of action. There are also times when you need the measured responsiveness of considered action and embodied listening. These help you make good decisions that require more than a moment's reaction time and account for longer-term consequences. For example, you wouldn't throw away your tea kettle on a whim because you burned your finger. Next time, you would pause and realize you need to handle it more carefully. As you progress as a somatic learner, you have more access to the ability to be responsive.

The process of getting to know your own nervous system happens over time. If you're like my clients, you probably wish you would never get triggered or be anxious, and that you would always be calm and centered. That is a completely human desire, but you actually need variety in your inner experience to keep things feeling alive. We'll look more at triggers in chapter 7, but for now I'm inviting you to start to notice that you have a nervous system that responds to stimuli.

You Operate Your Nervous System

The events taking place at any moment in your nervous system dramatically affect your experience. Let's look at your nervous system in a bit more detail to help you understand your body better.

Your nervous system is constantly moving between two states: activation or upregulation, which means your sympathetic nervous system is at work; and downregulation and calm, which means your parasympathetic nervous system is in the lead. You need both of these states. Movement and rest. Inhale and exhale. Wake and sleep. Fluctuating states are healthy. Staying in just one state or the other all the time isn't good for us.

A regulated nervous system moves naturally between upregulation and downregulation. Dr. Dan Siegel describes a regulated nervous system as operating with a "window of tolerance," which is the optimal state of arousal or stimulation in which we're able to function and thrive in everyday life. When your nervous system is operating within this window, you can learn effectively, play, and relate well to yourself and others.

When your system perceives a threat, it reacts to protect you. These somatic survival reactions are fully automatic and happen without your conscious choice. When you're triggered, you are having a survival reaction. When your amygdala perceives a threat—regardless of whether the threat is real—it sends a message to your body to react by fighting or fleeing. Sometimes both signals are sent; when this happens, your confused brain freezes, like a deer in the headlights. It's important to understand that these survival reactions originate in your brain and are ultimately there to keep you safe.

Your window of tolerance is an indication of what your nervous system can handle without becoming flooded or triggered. When you're triggered, you are no longer within your window of tolerance.

When you move outside that window, you become either hyperaroused or hypoaroused. Hypoarousal results from the freeze or collapse response, in which you shut down or dissociate. This can present in life as exhaustion, depression, flat affect, numbness, and disconnection. Hyperarousal results from the fight-or-flight response and is characterized by excessive activation. It can present as irritability, difficulty with concentrating, panic, constant anxiety, or being easily scared or startled. These states can be temporary, but they can also often linger if your system doesn't return to within your window of tolerance.

One example of hyperaroused dysregulation is anxiety—an upregulated, can't-feel-calm state. For many people, this is the constant way they experience themselves. Their nervous system has gotten stuck in the "on" position, and they feel a low-level fear or nervousness most or all of the time. True relaxation is challenging. For people in this state, work is typically soothing because it gives them something to do. The constant state of upregulation can be adrenalizing and addictive but also depleting.

Learning to regulate your own nervous system is a practice. It's not something most of us are taught. Many people attempt to self-regulate through the use of an external substance or a physical activity. They may reach for a cigarette or a drink when they want to feel calmer, or they might go for a run. But there are ways to work with your nervous system that require nothing but your attention. You start by noticing what's happening in your system. Are you feeling activated? Are you feeling calm?

Developing the skills of coming back to a calm center is not about being some enlightened master. It's about becoming empowered to have a life that you feel your best in. You can create a window of tolerance that feels calm and good. You don't need to live your life at the whim of your dysregulated nervous system, but getting there takes work. A significant benefit of embodiment is the ability to determine the quality of your internal experience. You get to decide what feels good inside your own experience. You get to practice being well in all the ways that matter most to you. How do you want to feel most of the time in your life? Are you ready to be responsible for that? If so, a trauma-informed practitioner grounded in neuroscience can be quite helpful. Nervous systems are healable.

Truth: you are alone inside your body. You get to learn how to operate your nervous system. You get to learn to create internal states that feel good to you. One significant way you can work with your nervous system to regulate it is by practicing specific breathing patterns. A little later we'll discuss some additional techniques that can influence your inner state.

PRACTICE MOMENT: How Is Your System?

One part of developing somatic awareness is learning to track what's happening inside of you. By doing this, you're paying attention to your nervous system. For this practice, which will only take a few minutes, it will help if you're in a quiet, private environment. The goal is merely to notice what is.

- Turn your attention toward what's happening inside. You can close your eyes if you wish. What sensations do you notice?

- Are you feeling any emotions?

- Can you notice what your energy feels like inside? Do you feel calm? Nervous? Amped up? Sleepy?

- Do you notice any impulses? Do you want to move around? Are you thirsty?

- When you stop and notice your inner world, what surprises you?

- Instead of asking, "Why am I feeling this way?" ask, "How am I feeling?" and "What else am I noticing?" Pause to gather the information that arises in response.

When you notice what you feel without judging or changing it, you can get curious about it. Stay with what you observe long enough to be interested instead of moving away from the feeling.

Internal Safety

Let it be clear that learning to self-regulate is a *process*. It takes a lifetime to develop mastery. Fortunately, we do have good guides for this journey. Zen master Thich Nhat Hanh speaks of the value of feeling calm internally when facing the hardest parts of life. Buddhists call this balanced internal state equanimity. Once you decide constant dysregulation isn't worth it, the inside of you can become an excellent place to dwell.

Presumably, you want your home to be a safe place to live; but have you considered that your body also needs to feel safe? Your body needs to be protected from outside threats. Your body also needs to be protected from internal threats. Choosing to work with your nervous system does *not* mean you won't have emotions. You'll still get thrown off-center. You won't magically avoid conflict. Those things are part of being human. But you will become a safe place to live.

Internal threat comes from the parts of you that are:

- self-critical
- hateful
- disrespectful
- mean
- bullying

Additional threats arise from the parts that:

- say unkind or nasty things about yourself, aloud or internally
- disregard the value of your work
- repeat harmful narratives about your worth

Even if you do all the work of becoming embodied, if you don't create internal safety, you won't want to feel inside of yourself. Who wants to hang out with a bully? Who wants to spend time with someone who constantly criticizes them—even if it's you, criticizing yourself? One definition of safety that I love is "having the agency to act on your own behalf." Many people lack a felt sense of safety, and they conflate safety with comfort; so it's important to build genuine inner safety.

If you haven't come across the Internal Family Systems (IFS) model yet, it's a helpful tool for understanding how internal safety works. The model proposes that you have a Self, who is wise, loving, and kind. Your Self is characterized by the eight *C*s: compassion, curiosity, clarity, creativity, calm, confidence, courage, and connectedness. You have all of your various parts, each of which is trying to do a specific job. Often these parts have arisen from survival strategies. For example, if you have a survival strategy of appeasement, the part of you that appeases is trying to keep you safe.

The parts of you who are mean to you are also trying to do a job. In their twisted way, they are actually trying to take care of you and keep you safe. They need healing and integration, not excisement. Creating internal safety often means working with a great therapist who can help you see the impact of these strategies and make different choices in the moment. But even without a therapist, there are plenty of ways we can help ourselves be kinder and gentler to ourselves.

As opposed to many other therapeutic models, IFS holds that each individual can access the eight *C*s without having to build them in therapy. The Self also knows how to heal and be there for all parts of ourselves. It is your Self that can help you create internal safety. Essentially, your Self can be a loving, supportive adult who helps all the scared and angry parts to feel heard, without allowing them to run the show.

Even when you're embodied, you won't always be calm and free of stress. That's not the goal. But you can learn to soothe yourself in hard moments. You can learn to *be with* difficult feelings in a more easeful way. Mastering the art of downregulation and learning to relax will help you create internal safety, which in turn helps you feel better and live longer—and be a better boss.

PRACTICE MOMENT: Feel Safe Inside

For this practice, you'll need at least ten to fifteen minutes in a quiet, comfortable, and physically safe environment where you won't be interrupted. You can close your eyes if you want, and put your body into a comfortable position.

To the extent that you can, invite relaxation. This means adjusting your body and your breathing to what feels relaxing and right to you.

Take some time to think about things you love that create a sense of safety for you: places, people, objects, situations. Once you feel the support of those, invite your most loving and supportive Self to come to the forefront.

Don't worry about how your Self shows up. Trust that it is exactly right.

You can now ask to receive compassion from yourself. You may wish to say this out loud, even if it feels a little silly.

"Can I receive compassion please?" is a simple way to phrase it.

Notice how it feels to receive compassion from yourself.

This practice is about feeling safe inside, so ask for that as well.

"Can I feel safe inside please?"

Then just notice what happens.

What surprises you right now?

What do you notice?

Stay with the feelings as long as you like.

To complete this practice, you may choose to commit to being safe inside yourself today. Try saying this phrase, either aloud or internally: "I commit to self-kindness today."

When any parts of you say things that don't feel kind, your Self can respond with something like, "Thank you for offering your care today."

Your Powerful B.B.O.D.Y.

You feel yourself by directing your attention to yourself. It's the quality of the presence that is essential. You want to have a direct experience of your inner world without your brain chattering about what's happening, what it means, and why you are experiencing it. Our brains are always trying to create meaning, and sometimes that's not helpful. With practice, we can access feeling as a pure experience without interpretation, narrative, or judgment.

When you feel yourself in this way, you have greater access to:

- longings and desires
- truth
- deep knowing
- knowing where you are (i.e., being here and now)
- knowing who you are
- your needs
- your boundaries
- discernment

A powerful tool to help you feel yourself is the acronym B.B.O.D.Y. It stands for:

Breathe

Bring it down to the ground

Observe your inner state

Dimensions and center

Yawn, stretch, and wiggle

Breathe

Breath is a crucial component in nervous system regulation. The easiest access you have to your nervous system is through your breath. When you're excited (upregulated), you breathe more quickly. When you're deeply relaxed (downregulated), your breathing slows. You can use your breath to intentionally create change in the state of your nervous system. Slowing and deepening your breath helps you slow down. Specifically, focusing on a longer exhale tells your nervous system to calm down. This can be particularly powerful for people with anxiety. When we're anxious, we're often told to take a deep breath. This instruction causes many people to focus on the inhale, which actually triggers the sympathetic nervous system and the body's fight-or-flight response, often making the anxiety worse. Focusing on and elongating the exhale is what triggers the parasympathetic nervous system, which regulates the body's rest functions.

PRACTICE MOMENT: Try Breathing Now

Without changing your breath, notice how you're breathing. Is it slow and deep, or shallow and quick? How does your body want to breathe if given a choice?

Here are two different breath practices you can try. See which one works better right now. These and other breath practices can be powerful tools in helping your nervous system return to a regulated state.

- **The 7/11 Breath:** Inhale for a count of seven. Exhale for a count of eleven. Repeat for a few minutes until you feel complete.

- **The Belly Breath:** Breathe fully into your belly. Imagine the breath moving low and deep into your body, not getting stuck in your chest. Your shoulders are not moving upward. Your belly is soft and expansive, and you can feel and see it move as breath gently enters and leaves. Do this for as long as you want.

Bring It Down to the Ground

Grounding is a nourishing somatic practice of downregulating your nervous system. When you ground, you remember and feel your connection with your body and with the Earth. You can slow things down, giving yourself space to feel more. This is a reason many people feel more connected and alive when they're in nature. When you feel connected, you move with more skill and grace. Neuroscience talks about grounding as nervous system regulation—more specifically, dorsal vagal regulation.

When you ground, you bring yourself to the here and now. You bring yourself to your body, to the place you are in this moment. You draw resources from that connection with yourself and Earth instead of from your nervous energy. Grounding is an act of deep self-love. It is a practice of belonging to yourself and to the Earth.

You might not be able to sit next to a mossy forest stream on your lunch break, but grounding is always available when you need to take your stress level down a notch. Grounding practice is helpful when things feel like they're going too fast, when you feel yourself at maximum capacity, when you're reeling. Simply find a private place, preferably with a door you can close, like your office, the bathroom, or even your car. Imagine your energy dropping into the cool, dense Earth beneath you. Allow your attention to carry you down into the dark and peaceful quiet. This is a great gift to give yourself when facing a troublesome situation at work. You deserve the time and space to create a special moment only for you.

It may feel like your work is so intense and demanding that this practice is unavailable. Maybe you think if you took time out of your day to do this, the rest of your day would fall apart. I had a client who was an emergency room doctor—probably one of the most demanding and high-stress jobs there is. She spent her days moving from crisis to crisis and rarely even ate on her shifts. It was common for her not even to take a bathroom break. She was in my office because the stress of her job had caused illness in her body. When I suggested she set the alarm on her phone and take a five-minute break each shift, she told me that was impossible. I invited her to try the practice for one week, and she agreed. A week later, she told me that some of her symptoms had lessened and that work had felt a little easier that week.

I understand the objections of people like my client who are convinced that the demands of their high-powered jobs mean they can't possibly take a short grounding break. But I assure you, you can. And you should. You will come to respect the power of grounding and the strength it gives you, and it will most likely help you do your job even better.

In the grounding technique shared in the Practice Moment below, you allow your energy and thinking to slow and drop downward as you imagine the Earth holding them. There are many ways to ground; this particular grounding practice utilizes your connection with the planet. Typically, grounding helps you feel calmer and more centered. When you take a pause to bring yourself here and now, any urgency you're experiencing usually lessens. When it feels impossible to slow down and ground, that's often when you need to do it the most.

PRACTICE MOMENT: Bring It Down to the Ground

For this practice, it's helpful to be standing and to have some quiet and privacy. If you would like, you can download the grounding meditation provided on my website, which is listed in the "Resources" section in the back of the book.

Begin by using your felt sense to notice what your energy is doing in your body. Can you feel where your energy is and how it is or isn't moving? Can you feel the speed at which your system moves? Don't try to change anything; just notice what is.

Be still and feel the connection between your body and your Earth home. Feel the action of gravity working on your body. Try to allow your skeleton to hold 5 percent more of your weight. Surrender your breath, and let yourself be breathed. Release all effort.

Imagine a cord of connection emerging from you that is as wide as your body at its widest point. Then imagine dropping that connecting cord downward into the heart of the Earth. Sink this imaginary root deep, deep down. Tell yourself silently that you are worthy of feeling calm, loved, and grounded.

Slow and deepen your breathing. Visualize your taproot moving downward, through the layers of the Earth's crust, deep into the planet's center. Feel for the regenerating energy of the molten core of the Earth. Allow any stress you're holding to move down your cord into the Earth, where the Earth can recycle it for you. Allow your excess energy and anxiety to be slowly absorbed and held by the Earth.

Take all the time you need to ground fully.

If you feel drained and need a resource, feel the energy there at the core of the Earth. That same fire that recycled your stress and anxiety can be a source of new, refreshed energy. Visualize using your taproot to pull some of that energy up into you. Allow it to move up your body and spill out the top of your head. Allow the Earth to nourish you.

Take a moment to feel into the ways grounding is a reciprocal relationship with Earth. You both give and receive sustenance. You love, and you are loved back.

Now notice your system. Has anything shifted? How do you feel now?

Observe Your Inner State

Another foundational somatic embodiment practice is observing. When you observe, you take a moment to direct your attention toward your body, without judgment. With neutral, gentle curiosity, you allow your attention to notice what is happening inside you. The key is to not be mean to yourself for what you notice. Simply accept what is, in this moment. You are caring about your inner world by turning your attention there. It is crucial to cultivate a kind attitude toward yourself.

You have already practiced observation earlier in this chapter when you practiced noticing your system. Observing allows insight into what's happening for you.

PRACTICE MOMENT: Observe Your Inner State

First, start with an intention: "I will notice what is going on in my body." Imagine pouring your attention into your body, starting at either your crown or feet. As you move your awareness through each area of your body, notice what is, without judgment. Gently ask yourself:

- What is tight?
- What feels spacious?
- What hurts?
- What feels pleasurable?
- What emotions do I feel?
- How's my mood?

Give each body part some attention. Notice any information coming from that part. The observing practice can take an hour, or it can take ten seconds. It all depends on how much time you have to practice. The longer you have to practice, the deeper you'll go, but a little is always better than none at all.

I have taught many people the practice of observing. More than a handful have told me they can't feel anything at first—no sensation, no emotion. It's frustrating for them to turn their attention inward and not get any information. If you try this practice a few times and get nothing, don't worry. It might not be the proper practice, or the proper practice right now. There are many other ways to practice.

You can keep up the practice of observing, and as you do, more information will come with time. Or you can let go of this practice and revisit it later. Some people love to observe and scan their body like this. They get a lot of information that way. But each person's body speaks to them differently. The thing all bodies have in common is that they don't speak in words. They speak in sensations, emotions, and desires.

While noticing what is happening inside, many folks get curious about why it's happening. "Why is my stomach contracted?" or "Why do I have this tension?" While this is a completely normal response, it is not the most helpful one. When you ask "Why?" you are essentially saying, "If I could only understand this, I won't have to feel like this anymore." But it doesn't work like that. Understanding why you feel what you feel will not make it go away.

Asking "why" is your brain trying to draw connections and make meaning. This isn't bad or wrong, but there isn't always meaning to be made. Sometimes "why" is about blaming yourself for feeling what you're feeling. Instead, stay out of participating in your own pathology. When I felt that contraction in my shoulder, I convinced myself it would stop if I could understand why it happened. I wanted to be "fixed." It took a lot of holding and releasing that shoulder to realize that "why" didn't matter. I had a shoulder contraction. That is what was. Understanding why it was there would not shift it. Believing in my brokenness wasn't helpful. It interfered with my healing.

Asking why is far less valuable than asking *what*:

- What's happening?
- What am I noticing?
- What is my energy doing?
- What does this part of me need?

These are all helpful questions for observing.

Observing is a technique you can use multiple times each day, at any time. It's especially beneficial when you feel tense or irritated, or when you notice something just feels off. Any time you need to, take a moment to turn your attention toward yourself. Gather information about what you're feeling and what information your body is offering. When I do this, I often see that I have a need I've ignored or that there's something I need to say that I haven't said. You can always ask yourself, "What do I need right now?"

Dimensions and Center

Do you feel three-dimensional? Think about it: how many dimensions do you typically inhabit? Many of my clients report feeling that they exist in only two dimensions—length and width. They feel like flat cutouts of themselves.

Trauma in particular can make you feel two-dimensional. This makes sense if you consider that trauma is a wound to the body. It keeps the victim stuck in certain moments in time, in certain reactions. What is lost is the capacity for spontaneity, for play, for curiosity. Life without those elements is pretty flat, yes? One of the signature signs of dissociation is a kind of numbness that prevents you from feeling like a three-dimensional body moving in space. Instead, your physical experience seems to lack depth. It can lack nuance. As you heal from trauma, one of the things that can happen is that you begin to inhabit yourself more fully.

If you ever feel two-dimensional, the following practice will be helpful, albeit challenging. Embodiment is about fullness of form. It is about being present. You exist within a grounded and settled form. You are not an empty shell. You have three dimensions: length, width, and depth.

PRACTICE MOMENT: Practice of Three Dimensions

I learned the practice of three dimensions from my somatic coach, Meredith Broome. It is typically a standing practice, but it can be a sitting practice as well, depending on your ability. The following instructions will walk you through feeling each of your length, width, and depth dimensions, eventually landing at your center, which is where you are when you feel your whole self.

Length

As you stand, first explore and feel into your length. This dimension goes up and down your spine, back body, and full height, allowing you to be upright in the world. Here you invite in your self-respect through your grace.

You allow your skeleton to do the work it is designed to do. Your structure holds up your body. You let your weight rest on your bones. You settle onto your frame. There is both a settling down toward Earth and a lifting toward the sky. Your breath expands your lungs in the vertical plane, and your lungs expand to a fuller capacity.

Check and notice your back body here, which extends the entire length of your spine—that vast expanse of skin and structure that is half of your height. Stand pressed backward against a wall if pressure would help you feel your back body more. Explore that sensation. Notice how feeling your full length gives you access to knowing your value, your healthy pride.

Take a few steps around, noticing how you can move with your length. Observe that you can move around the space you're in with your full length intact. This natural lifting upward brings you to presence with yourself. There's no need to force it; you instead find what is easy and effortless. Claim the space of your height, every millimeter. Your spine is relaxed and easy, pliant and movable. Being in your length means you have access to your flexibility. Your spine is fluid and tall at the same time.

Width

When your exploration of your length feels complete, turn your attention to your width. This is the total space you take up from one side to the other. First, feel your edges—the edges of your arms, legs, torso, and head. Next, move inward toward inhabiting your full width. Alternately, you can unfurl from your midline out toward your edges. Play with both, noticing which one feels more right at this moment. To support this exploration, allow your breath to get wide; take breaths that fill your lungs to their side edges. Use your imagination as needed.

Pour yourself into your physical container, filling your body up to the edges. Notice here how expanding into your full width expands your openness and availability. How can you connect with others as you widen and include them in your perspective? Width is all about spreading out, taking up your rightful space, and being in good connection. Spread into your somatic width, fill yourself out to your edges, and get wide.

Your width is where you can hold paradox, complication, and nuance. You release the midline contraction and spread out. Take up the entire space of you. Notice if you allow your stomach to widen, your eyes, your calves. Widen across your shoulders and your chest. Expanding into width is the opposite of folding into yourself or armoring yourself in protection. Notice how you can take up your full width and feel safe simultaneously. Take a few steps and notice too how you can move around your space with your width, including a broader perspective. Movement is easier and more graceful when you are vast. Explore this for as long as it is interesting.

Depth

Next, you will add the dimension of depth. Find a good, easy stance and feel for your back body. Feel how your clothes touch your skin—the backs of your arms, torso, butt, legs. Like a body scan, slowly move your attention from your back, all the way through you, moving horizontally toward the front. Take your time and go slow. Allow the depth of your body to be felt. Appreciate how your skeleton, muscles, and internal organs work so hard for you.

When your attention reaches the front of you, see if you can maintain awareness of your full depth, all at the same time. Allow your lungs to expand, back to front, to support this dimension. Unclench any abdominal muscles you may be con-tracting, and allow yourself to be easy and expansive.

When you explore this plane of you, you welcome your past, present, and future. If you consider that linear Western culture orients toward time, you are standing solidly in your lin-eage, with your ancestors at your back and future generations stretching out ahead of you.

Notice how you can move about with your depth aware-ness; you don't need to stay still. This is your depth, the third dimension from your back body through your bones and your organs, through your fascia and other tissues, and all of the thickness of you, all the way toward the front of your body. This third dimension of depth is where you connect with everyone who has come before you and everyone who will come after. Explore this as long as you want.

Center

Now feel all your three-dimensionality at once. Become a three-dimensional being, filled with expansive three-dimensional breath. Feel the air shifting around you as you move with the fullness of your embodiment. Play with stillness and movement. Do this as long as you want.

Now, let it all go. Let go of paying attention. Let your mind go where it wants to go. Let your eyes see what they want to see. Forget about embodiment for a minute. Take a break.

And then see if you can bring it all back: length, width, depth, three-dimensionality, breath. It's a lot to pay attention to! And congratulations—you have found your center.

Feel into center as connection and presence with yourself. Take a moment to notice a feeling of groundedness and deeper access to your body and your brain's wisdom. In this place, you aren't triggered; you aren't reactive. You're operating holistically. Consider center as equilibrium—your baseline. It is a place you can return to whenever you want.

You are constantly moving on center and off-center. Getting thrown off-center is a normal part of being human. Perhaps you're taking a meditation class, and after the class is over you come out to your car feeling grounded, enjoying the sun on your skin. But then you get in your car and check your text messages. Your partner texted that you forgot to say goodbye to them when you left, and they feel hurt. And *wham,* you're off-center as you consider how your afternoon might now be different. Maybe you feel mad and resentful because you had been feeling so peaceful before. Sound familiar?

Center is not a place you reach in your emotions, where you are consistently calm and collected. Center does not mean you will never get upset or sad or angry. Center is who you are when you are at your best, regardless of what is happening around you or to you. You can feel the depths of grief and be entirely centered. When you're centered, you can make clear decisions and take decisive action.

There is no somatically enlightened place you can arrive at where you won't feel impacted by those around you. Feeling impact is a core piece of your humanity, whether the impact is unpleasant or extraordinary. You can get good at getting knocked off-center and then returning to center. Center is a place you come back to again and again. This is the practice. In the words of '90s rock band Chumbawamba: "I get knocked down, then I get up again. You're never gonna keep me down."

Getting knocked off-center happens to everyone. Each time you get knocked off-center is a practice opportunity for finding your way home to yourself. How often do you get knocked off-center during a typical work-day? If you're like most people, probably a lot.

All leaders make mistakes, even the most skilled. If you're a manager who models healthy human behavior, you acknowledge your mistakes when you make them. When you get knocked off-center, you can admit it. You can say, "Wow, that threw me for a loop. Give me a minute," or "Let me feel into that for a minute."

Transparency about your internal process is likely not high on your list of leadership skills you want to work on, especially if it means sharing with your employees. I'm not suggesting that your work relationships become focused on your emotions. What I do recommend is that you make room for yourself when you get knocked off-center. You're not impervious to impact, nor should you be. That's not healthy or human. When center eludes you, it's time to tend to yourself kindly, in whichever ways work best for you.

Yawn, Stretch, and Wiggle

Sound and movement complete your embodiment toolkit. When you make a sound, your vocal cords vibrate inside you, and you feel the reverberations of the sound you've produced. Making sound can support the regulation of your nervous system. Dr. Peter Levine, the founder of Somatic Experiencing therapy, suggests taking a full breath, then creating a low "vooooooooooo" sound to help your nervous system calm down. Yogic breath practice suggests making a buzzing sound like a bee. Try one or both now. What do you experience?

Movement is life moving through you. When you yawn, stretch, and wiggle, you allow your system to discharge excess energy and move anything that's stuck. When you move your body, even if only to make slight adjustments, the rest of you responds. At any moment, consider how you can make your physical experience 2 percent more comfortable. If you don't currently have a regular movement practice, take some time to ask your body how it would like to start moving. What movement brings you pleasure and aliveness?

You are probably already acutely aware that, as a boss, you're subject to burnout. A core component of supporting your mental health and avoiding burnout is movement. Making movement a priority is essential, but that doesn't have to mean exercise or cardio. The key is integrating movement into your life that you want to do and that feels right for you. Dancing in your chair? Great. Yoga is wonderful. Wrist rolls are perfect. Move just a little bit, or as much as you want. Ask your body, "How would you like to move right now?"

As we've discussed, a person can do movement practice without being present and embodied for it. I once had a client who ran marathons all over the world. When I asked him if he felt embodied as he ran, he said he didn't. After he experienced a significant repetitive strain injury, he gave embodied movement a go. He practiced focusing on his internal experience as he ran instead of checking out and listening to his earbuds. As he made his running practice an embodiment practice, his body started to talk with more frequency and nuance. He learned to tune into his body wisdom, and his running technique became one of somatic insight.

When you're moving, be present. Pay attention and feel. Whatever you're already doing to move your body can become an embodied practice: walking to your car, swimming, gardening, doing the dishes, walking the dog. Invite your attention and your noticing self. What are you feeling?

The natural state of your organism is to move and breathe freely. When you move and breathe more, you feel more. The same is true in reverse; when you move and breathe less, you feel less. Many people constrict their breath and movement as a way to manage feeling overwhelmed. If you notice you're resisting movement or breathing, be kind and don't judge. Remember that there are good reasons to want to feel less, but resistance to movement is also resistance to joy. When you turn down the volume on feeling, you turn it down across the board, not just in a specific area of your choosing. Not moving is a strategy for not feeling anything.

Any of your survival strategies can become a habitual state. You've likely known people who live their lives in a state of panic or trauma response. Maybe you've had a boss who was always angry and looking for a fight, or locked into the flight response of avoiding conflict. Survival responses can happen in a singular moment, but they can also become defining features in life.

Movement gives you the opportunity to move out of habituated states and become more fluid and responsive to the moment. If you're not moving much in your life and are resisting moving, you may be in an ongoing freeze response. It's time to listen and discover what you need: Quiet alone time? Support from a friend? Time in the natural world? Rest? Remember, resistance is an invitation to pay attention. One capacity of leadership is flexibility, or the ability to respond to new challenges. Having an embodied movement practice gives you a way to practice moving in mindful new ways.

PRACTICE MOMENT: Yawn, Stretch, and Wiggle

Take a moment to move your body in any way it wants to move. Often, music helps movement become uninhibited.

Give a shake. Wiggle your booty. Bounce up and down with your knees. The point is to move in ways that feel good. You can stretch if you like, or prance about like a unicorn in a parade. Move for the sake of pleasure.

Try it for ten to thirty seconds. When you're done, do a quick body scan. What do you notice?

B.B.O.D.Y. Cheat Sheet

B—Breathe. Notice your breathing. You don't need to change anything; just pay attention to your breath, without judgment. Has it been a while since you've taken a full breath? Ask your body how you want to breathe right now.

B—Bring it down to the ground. Ground yourself by connecting with the Earth. Drop your energy down. Downregulate your nervous system through breathing and grounding.

O—Observe. Observe your inner experience. Mindfully scan your body. Notice your body in space. Notice where it touches the ground. Notice internal contractions and internal ease. Observe how your energy is moving and how it connects.

D—Dimensions and center. Extend into your three dimensions. Feel your length, your width, your depth. Feel your edges and your solidity. Feel for center, connected with yourself. Ask yourself, "Is there anything I need?

Y—Yawn, stretch, and wiggle. How can you make your physical experience 2 percent more comfortable? How can you access 2 percent more of your felt sense? Embodiment includes breathing, feeling, and moving. So move! Yawning is a great reset for your breath and central nervous system.

B.B.O.D.Y. is a five-part practice that you can take everywhere you go and that you always have at your disposal. You can B.B.O.D.Y. any time, anywhere, for any length of time— four seconds, or four hours.

You've been doing a lot of somatic work in this book so far. In the next chapter, we'll move our focus to working with your brain and psyche.

Chapter 4 Takeaways

O You can learn to operate your specific nervous system.

O You can create internal safety by being kind to yourself.

O Foundational embodiment practices include breath, grounding, observing, getting three-dimensional, centering, and moving.

O The acronym B.B.O.D.Y. helps you remember how to embody quickly.

O Being embodied is all about practicing being embodied.

PART II

EMBODIED

LEADERSHIP

IN

ACTION

5

INHABIT YOUR POWER!

I'LL LET YOU IN on a secret: I have a tail. And if you're a boss, you do too. We have huge, massive dragon tails. The problem is that we don't even know it most of the time. Imagine walking down the street while behind you is a wide swath of destruction, wrought by your tail. Small cars, delivery vans, entire garbage trucks are gone. It doesn't stop there. If you slow down and look, you'll notice that the whole town where you live has been demolished. Lives destroyed. Fortunes abandoned. And all because you have this colossal tail that you're dragging over everything without noticing the impact.

Creating mayhem and destruction was pretty much my experience of becoming a boss. Becoming a leader wasn't just added hours and responsibilities; the thing I somehow missed was the power I suddenly had. But just because I was in charge, that didn't mean I knew how to wield power with grace. At first I didn't acknowledge my new organizational power. I didn't feel any different. I still felt like me.

One day, after receiving some harsh feedback from an employee about my lack of management skills, I had a session with my somatic coach. I described my confusion to my coach. Why was my employee acting like I was "the Man"? Why did they expect me to take care of their needs? Why were they pissed about the lack of internal communication in the company? My coach gently explained to me the phenomenon of my tail. She said I had gone from being a regular old human to a mighty, giant dragon overnight. My employee was angry because I was the one with the power in the situation, and they expected me to use it accordingly. In other words, they expected me to behave like a leader—because I was one!

Coming into power can catch you unawares. Like most folks, you've been living your life, complaining about bosses, watching as they messed up. Now suddenly you're the one people are watching. They complain about you! Coming to know your own power and directing it skillfully takes some doing.

People in Power Suck . . . or So I Thought Until It Was Me

I grew up queer in a Rust Belt town at the end of the Reagan era. No one was teaching my friends and me how to be emotionally fluent. No one said, "This is how you feel yourself." We learned to feel the edges of our bodies at punk shows, in filthy underground venues, through a fog of cigarette smoke and cheap beer.

As hardcore bands took the cramped stages, we slammed our bodies into each other in the mosh pit. We committed to feeling something, anything, through the violent pounding and stomping. Injuries abounded, but so did care. When one of us would sneak up onto the stage and then dive off bravely into the crowd, the rest of us would catch them . . . most times. They would float on the top of the group for a few moments, then be gently brought back down to the ground. We cared for each other in our outsider community because no one else did.

I grew up with no good role models of power and leadership. All around me, the examples of leadership I saw were corrupt, exploitative, and fraught with massive ego. Many of us had parents who denied our humanity while turning a blind eye to the trauma we were experiencing. We had unreasonable teachers and school principals who didn't care. Armed drug dealers who sold us meth, telling us not to worry because it "wasn't crack." College professors who played favorites and slept with students. All the sleazy and unkind bosses we had at minimum-wage jobs. I had friends who enlisted in the military, were abused by their superior officers, and were sent into armed conflict. I watched friends die, as if they were an expendable resource. Yep, everyone who had power over us completely sucked. Power was terrible, and those who had it were heartless jerks.

After all those poor examples of people in power, I knew I could do it better. Part of starting a company was proving that people like me could hold power. You know those people who don't have kids but who have plenty of opinions about how everyone should parent? That was me when I started my company. My organization would deeply respect each employee! Treat our workers with care and kindness! And pay them well! I thought I would know exactly how to do it all right after spending my life watching everyone do it wrong.

With that dream in full swing, I totally missed it when the power tail sprouted. I didn't notice that there was a new appendage trailing behind me, bursting with untrained strength. Before I knew it, I had left a trail of hurt and angry people in my wake.

When you first step into being a boss, everything is unprecedented. You're learning to lead, and you're doing it in front of an audience. Your employees are watching—and being affected by—your every move. One employee in my company who left early said, "Yes, I understand that you're learning to be a boss. I have compassion for that. But I don't want to be your guinea pig while you learn." Fair enough.

Your tail only becomes an asset after you learn to operate it. Once you've embodied your power, you can use that tail to shelter and protect those in your care. You can skillfully demolish, leverage, rebuild, and wield your authority like a *boss* boss whom people love to work with.

If you are a boss, have ever been a boss, or think you might want to be a boss, you have my most profound respect. Leading is *hard*. Everybody thinks you sit around making calm, cool, informed decisions, but you know the truth.

Your job is to create an environment where employees feel safe enough to be productive. You must create a satisfying work culture so they want to stay. You have to retain your talent while meeting your revenue goals. Also important are your own satisfaction and joy.

As a boss, I have evolved from my young punk days of assuming all power was terrible, and I've realized that power is not inherently bad at all. You just need to know how to use it with skill. You can hold power responsibly, sustainably, and confidently without being a tyrant. We badly need influential leaders who can guide humanity to a more sustainable way of life.

Now is a crucial time if you have recently sprouted a dragon tail (i.e., been promoted to a leadership position). You're trying to learn to lead in front of everybody! Those you're leading are watching you out of the corner of their eye: will you do a good job? Or will you be another asinine manager who makes their jobs and lives more difficult?

What Power Is

The crux of this book is how to hold your power with skill and grace. To effectively embody your power, you must first have a good understanding of what power is. This next part may be a bit heady, but your head is part of your body, and having an understanding of power and power dynamics is essential to your leadership.

So what exactly is power? The typical definition of power is the authority to change an outcome or influence others. Another definition of power I learned from Miki Kashtan is that power equals access to internal and external resources to meet needs. So here's my definition: power is both your ability to choose your response to situations, and your ability to direct or influence the behavior of others. It also includes your internal and external access to the resources you require to meet your needs.

People want to have power so they can meet their needs. Having power gives you access to meeting your needs. That's pretty simple. You can obtain power in lots of different ways, and likewise, you have lots of choices about how you use it.

More broadly, having power means you can effectively use the influence you have access to. You wield authority based on personal certainty. You develop the confidence to make effective decisions for yourself and others. You build tolerance for taking risks. You believe you know a good path forward, and you effectively communicate that vision to others.

Types of Power

Generally speaking, there are two types of power: formal and informal.

Formal power is power given by a role, position, or title. In hierarchical power structures, formal power may be identified as a source of power, but it is actually only one facet within a complex web of power relationships. Many new leaders assume that because formal power is bestowed upon them when they take the role, they hold authority. This is not true. You may have institutional authority, but that does not mean your employees will follow your lead or that you will be able to influence them positively. That requires informal power.

Informal power, or social power, comes in four types that are distinguished by how each is derived.

Majority

This type of power derives from belonging to a majority of identity or a similar community. For example, in a space where the majority of people are from Mexico, there is power in the shared identity of being from Mexico. Majority power is situational, meaning that it only exists in certain contexts.

Systemic

Systemic power is derived from laws, policies, customs, or institutions established for the benefit of a particular group. In North America, whiteness is the norm of culture, resulting in great benefit to those with white skin.

Relational

Relational power comes from who you know and the access you have to people who have any type of power.

Experiential

Experiential power is derived from your body of knowledge and lived experience. This is the power of being an expert in a topic.

It's important to note that relational and experiential power are both earned. They contribute greatly to a felt sense of "power-within," a certain type of power we'll discuss in a moment.

Your identities affect how much access you have to both formal and informal power. Some identities give more access to societal power (i.e., privilege). Privilege can be defined as access to unearned power. Those with identities that give them less access to power often have to work harder to feel their power. This is unfair, and I empathize.

It has taken some doing for me to feel my power as a queer, nonbinary trans, fat, female-socialized person. Becoming embodied takes intention and practice, and as a result of my experience, I am so grateful I relearned how to feel. It made my path to swinging that dragon tail with style and grace easier. I could feel it when I was messing up; I could feel it when I was getting it right. Ultimately, being able to feel your power is what will effectively guide your leadership.

Different Ways of Using Power

There are four different ways of using power, and it's worth considering which of these you'll base your leadership in. My understanding of power is informed by Starhawk's analysis (for more information, see Starhawk's books listed in the "Resources" section at the end of the book). Each definition is followed by an example.

Power-Over

For a long time, power-over was the only kind of power many people were able to recognize. Power-over is based on domination or control, often using fear, coercion, and oppression as tools. Power-over is why many who might be excellent bosses shy away from leadership. They don't want to use that kind of power or be those kinds of people. Power-over is why I hated people in authority for a long time. When someone uses their power over you, it sucks to be on the receiving end.

Power-over relies on taking and lack of consent. Boundaries are disregarded. Decisions get made without considering the impact on all involved. No one loves feeling powerless, and those who suffer as a result of somebody exercising power-over will often resort to using power-under as a counter-measure (see discussion of power-under below).

In her book *Truth or Dare,* Starhawk writes:

> Power-over enables one individual or group to make the decisions that affect others, and to enforce control. This power is wielded from the workplace, in the schools, in the courts, in the doctor's office. It may rule with weapons that are physical or by controlling the resources we need to live: money, food, medical care; or by controlling more subtle resources: information, approval, love. We are so accustomed to power-over, so steeped in its language and its implicit threats, that we often become aware of its functioning only when we see its extreme manifestations.

For example, imagine Mike, a facility manager for a craft brewery who supervises a team of eighteen workers. He uses both his formal and informal power in aggressive ways. For example, when an employee tells him there is a problem with a piece of equipment due to another employee's negligence, Mike tells the whistleblower: "Just fix the problem. I don't need to hear about what you think other people did wrong." In another example, Mike decides to dock an employee's pay when they miss work because their partner was in a car accident. Mike is using power-over.

Power-Under

Power-under means acting in covert resistance to power structures. In the workplace, this can include talking smack, gossip, and complaining without taking action. Power-under is a maladaptive response to power-over. Sometimes power-under is the best a person can do if they can't find their way to their power or are actively prohibited from doing so. Power-under seeks to disrupt, be divisive, and subvert power-over.

Michelle is the lead medical assistant for a busy medical practice. She's responsible for managing the calendar for all the medical assistants. She dislikes her boss, the clinical director, who is always in a rush and isn't responsive in a timely manner when Michelle has questions or needs. Instead of taking her concerns to her boss, Michelle often gossips with the other medical assistants about how terrible her boss is. Michelle is using power-under.

Power-With

Power-with is shared power. This is one of the kinds of power I hope you want to embody. This is the power of collaboration and sharing ideas. Influence moves multidirectionally, meaning you influence your employees, and they influence you. Power-with helps you build organizations that don't rely on domination to be profitable or successful. Because employees have power, they have buy-in.

Power-with enables big, beautiful group projects to succeed. Power-with does not mean that all decisions are made by majority vote or consensus. Leadership is still needed. Someone needs to steer the ship and provide direction, but the leader who uses power-with creates a culture based on the shared understanding that everyone's work adds value.

Starhawk describes power-with as "the power of a strong individual in a group of equals, the power not to command, but to suggest and be listened to, to begin something and see it happen."

Power-with lets you build teams where all group members communicate respectfully with each other, and where the leader conscientiously makes an effort to refrain from using power-over. When the leader does make unilateral decisions, they acknowledge the inherent power differential. Team members are empowered to make decisions within their sphere of responsibility.

Devaughn is the director of development at a small nonprofit devoted to helping youth acquire skills and work experience in the media industry. The company's mission includes working collaboratively. Devaughn manages a team of eight. In their weekly meeting, each person is given time to speak about the four standing agenda items: what they've accomplished in the past week, what they'll work on this week, what support they need, and how they feel things are going. Each person gets equal time to share, so that all voices are heard. When a team member mentions something challenging, Devaughn schedules a meeting with them to hear more. Devaughn also has developed a mentoring program for his staff, and he meets with each of them monthly to support them professionally. Devaughn is using power-with.

Power-Within

Power-within is your personal power. It's when you have the dreams, the gumption, the grit, and the internal support to do what you want to do in the world. Power-within means having self-respect and valuing your worth. When you act from a place of power-within, you honor yourself and others while simultaneously getting stuff done.

Power-within is self-mastery. You are skilled in responsiveness, as opposed to reactivity. Power-within is what allows you to lead responsibly, sustainably, and effectively. As a leader, your power comes from within, from your presence. Presence comes from embodiment. To tap into your full capacity, you inhabit your body. Power-within is what people observe when they decide to follow your leadership. It's responsible to note here that power-within is confidence, and that arriving at personal confidence means you've done a lot of work. This can be indicative that you've had access to time, resources, and energy to devote to your own learning and growth. I say this to acknowledge that the opportunity to develop power-within is a privilege.

Tasya manages a team of housing-rights lawyers protecting tenants' rights. An attorney herself, Tasya has had a regular meditation practice for years. Sitting in meditation has given Tasya the ability to be with herself no matter what the situation is. When she meets with her team, she mostly listens as they discuss the challenges they're facing. When she speaks, her voice has a resonating and calming effect on the group. They often take her suggestions seriously. Tasya is using power-within.

PRACTICE MOMENT: Assessing Your Power

I want you (and everyone) to have access to internal and external resources to meet your needs; that is, I want you to have power. Having power is a good thing, and it's even better to know it when you have it.

Having power and feeling it don't always happen simultaneously. This means you can have access to a lot of power and not feel it—or even know it.

In this practice, you'll do a self-reality check about the level of power you currently have access to. This exercise utilizes your mind and power of analysis more than your felt sense.

Grab your writing device. You'll need about ten minutes of uninterrupted quiet time.

Do a quick B.B.O.D.Y. to prepare yourself, taking no more than a minute.

Ask yourself the following questions, and record your answers.

Formal power: In my current position, what formal power do I have access to, bestowed by my title or position?

Informal power:

- **Majority:** In my current position, am I part of a majority group in my workplace (race, gender, age, body type, sexual orientation, etc.)? Do I hold identities that are held by a majority of those around me?

- **Systemic:** In my current position, how do I benefit from company policies, norms, or customs put into place to support people like me?

- **Relational:** In my current position, how do I benefit or have I benefited from my relationships with or access to people with power?

- **Experiential:** In my current position, how do I benefit or have I benefited from my learning or lived experience?

After you've reflected on these questions, notice how you feel or don't feel the power you hold. There's no need to adjust or fix anything. This is an assessment you can do at any time, since power is always in flux.

Wielding Power with Clarity and Grace Comes from Practice

Which of your managers or bosses have used their gigantic dragon tails for good? Which ones have uplifted those around them and were not afraid to say no—but did so with compassion? Effective leaders pay attention to every person they lead. They figure out how best to develop, coach, and motivate them as individuals. Great leadership has a spirit of being in service to the team. This is how excellent leaders get tremendous results.

Years ago, I attended a workshop on mindful eating. The participants were doing hard, vulnerable work. There were two facilitators, Nil and Haley. Nil was the founder of the Buddhist and somatic retreat space we were meeting in, and Haley was his coteacher. The retreat space was right off a main street in downtown San Francisco. The chairs were arranged in a semicircle, and the two presenters took turns speaking at the front of the room.

After lunch, we reassembled, and there was a new student in the small audience of about twenty. When we were asked to describe our experience of eating lunch, people shared with authenticity. When it was the new student's turn, he declined to answer. He looked rough, and I guessed he was living on the streets. While we sat in the circle he exhibited some behaviors that were different from the rest of the group, such as sleeping in his chair and making odd movements and noises.

As this continued, members of the group became visibly distressed by the new student's presence. Haley seemed agitated and concerned, although Nil paid no attention. There was another round of sharing and, again, the new student refused to answer. Haley got upset and said, "Nil, I think we need to ask him to leave." Some people started to gather their things because they felt unsafe. I knew that what happened next would be pivotal.

Nil asked Haley if he could handle it. When she agreed, he turned toward the disruptive student. With care and firmness in his voice, Nil said, "We are all sharing right now. Part of being here is participating. You can leave if you don't wish to participate. You are also welcome to stay and share."

His tone of voice was level and warm. He embodied confidence. He spoke from a grounded presence and set a clear boundary that didn't exclude the new student, although he clearly stated the expectation that the student would have to participate if he wished to stay. When Nil spoke, I felt my system, as well as the room, relax. A leader had set a boundary with clarity and compassion. Nil gave the person encountering the boundary dignity and agency.

After Nil spoke to the student, he agreed to stop being disruptive. He apologized and left with his humanity intact. The workshop continued.

Most of what I remember from that workshop is that one potent moment. Nil showed me what it looks like when someone uses their power in a solid, kind, and professional manner. He gave that man, and the class, the power of presence.

Later I asked Nil about that moment. He could barely remember it. Nil is a somatic practitioner who works in a mental health ward. He has a lot of experience being present with people who have mental illness, and he does mindful somatic practice daily. His training and experience have given him an embodied presence. When he needs it, like in that workshop, that presence shows up effortlessly.

Embodying your power means that all the practice pays off at some point. Your body becomes the teaching. Your body becomes the leader. Nil didn't have to think to himself, "How should I handle this delicate moment that the workshop hinges on?" He moved and acted in alignment with his practiced values. Richard Strozzi-Heckler, founder of Strozzi Somatics, teaches that when you're under stress, your body reverts to your level of practice. Because Nil had had years of practice, he responded under pressure with love. He is a role model to me for wielding power well, with grace, clarity, and care.

Every day, you face situations where you can practice how you hold your power as a leader. How your body responds to difficult feedback, how you react to challenging impact—these events are part of how you lead. Employees are more aware of your inner world than you are of theirs; such is the power dynamic. They track you to determine how you'll react or respond and what kind of mood you're in. They're trying to determine how to be in your presence, how to feel safe. This happens even if you are the kindest boss in the world.

How you are matters to your employees. It's not what you're saying but how you're being. Have you ever asked someone how they're doing because you sensed something was wrong? Perhaps they responded, "I'm fine," through clenched teeth. Their words did not correspond with their tone of voice, body posture, and a thousand other signals. The same is true of you. You can pretend to be calm and centered while your body lets everyone know how you really feel. Or you can *practice* being calm and centered so you have a strong foundation to rest upon when stressful moments occur.

Holding power well as a boss is a tremendous balancing act. If your employees have not been in leadership positions before, they have no idea how challenging the role is. They look to you for guidance and leadership, as well as fairness. As a good boss, you recognize that your employees have the potential for as much power-within as you do. If you're a great boss, you help them realize that potential. But employees often don't feel empowered to say no to you. The imbalance this creates can lead to interesting problems.

Problems That Can Occur with Power

Most bosses can eventually learn to wield power with balance and care. But mistakes with power still happen, even for the most skilled leaders. Many of the problems with power that show up in interpersonal relationships (like marriage or partnership) also occur at work. Though power and hierarchy are often clearer to spot at work, the power problems explored here are common in all relationships.

Following is a list of some of the most common power problems:

- **You don't know how to listen.** Your employees don't feel heard, even though you think you listen.

- **You interrupt, talk over, or verbally dominate people.**

- **You value the input of some employees over others.**

- **You speak disrespectfully about an employee to anyone.**

- **You value your time above theirs.** Everyone's time is equal. Just because you have more power, that does not make the hours of your life worth more than anyone else's. Expecting employees to take work home or work during vacation exemplifies not valuing the time of others.

- **You disregard boundaries.** If they're on vacation, you text them regardless.

- **You're dismissive of their concerns.** "Oh, Rhoda always worries about the money," or "Antonio is so sensitive. It's not that big of a deal."

- **You flatten power.** You secretly believe stepping into your power means denying others theirs. You may feel guilty about holding power, and you may not want to use power-over. While attempting to share power, you inadvertently flatten it. This mindset holds that power is a limited resource and there is only so much to go around, so you think that being excellent and fair means divvying up the power pie into equal portions.

  While this appears to make sense on one level, consider the following example: instead of considering all ideas and then deciding based on your judgment, you go along with an employee's suboptimal idea in an attempt to share power. You want your employee to feel valued, and you don't want to seem bossy. However, by following the lead of a person who is not the leader, you flatten power between you. When you don't yet feel comfortable owning the power you have, you're willing to reduce your power to the level of someone else's. You have jumped the leader-ship. While this may make the employee feel good in the short term, it doesn't benefit the team as a whole in the long term. It could also backfire, with the employee being embarrassed by their idea failing, and the rest of the team losing faith in your judgment.

  In the real-life words of a person who wishes to remain anonymous but who gave permission to share their experience:

  > One of my most exploitative contracts came in the context of a boss who insisted they rejected traditional power dynamics and thought of us as peers. When I left and they asked for feedback about why, I said, "You can't treat me as a peer when you are the business owner and absorb all the profits of our work together. I can't perform with the passion of a co-owner, and it's not right of you to expect me to, when your hourly rates are ten times mine. I know you don't want to be a boss, but your attempts to reject the role just made an exploitative situation."

Flattening power is a natural mistake often born out of a desire to reject modern capitalism. It's something every small business owner who hires employees but wants to be ethical has to figure out how to navigate.

- **You forget that someone else's experience is real to them.** When an employee tells you about a negative situation they're experiencing, you judge the situation or them. You think they're exaggerating, you don't believe them, or you think they're just being a whiny baby. You think it would be different if you were in their shoes. Which is related to . . .

- **You listen through your lens.** You hear the words they're saying, but you don't take the opportunity to try to understand. You forget to empathize. Perhaps they're complaining about a coworker you like and value, so you tell them that person has the best intentions. Although this may feel true to you, you aren't acknowledging the truth they're sharing with you from their own experience.

- **You commit microaggressions.** You enact indirect, subtle, or unintentional discrimination against marginalized group members. Microaggressions are small statements or actions that reinforce oppressive systems. An example of a microaggression is telling a Black person in a tone of surprise or wonderment, "You are so articulate." You've had enough cultural training not to make overtly racist or sexist statements, but not enough so you can filter your harmful behaviors and words before they emerge.

- **You get annoyed when an employee expresses a need.** For example, a trans employee asking about gender-neutral bathroom signs irritates you. Instead of remembering their experience is real to them, you hear more work for you.

- **You forget that because of the power differential, your somatic survival response carries added weight when reacting to an employee.** For example, if your conditioned survival response is to fight, you get aggressive when triggered, and the aggression is amplified through the power dynamic. If you typically have flight responses under duress, you disappear without communication when triggered, and an employee is left alone to figure out what happened, which causes them not to trust that they can rely on you as a leader.

That's some of what can go wrong with holding power, but there are many more mistakes a leader can make. If you're unclear about whether you're making any mistakes with your power, it can be a great idea to ask your employees for feedback. Create a way for them to let you know anonymously how they think you're handling your management responsibilities. Your employees are the ones who can help you understand where you're holding power poorly. If they offer you the gift of this feedback, be wise and take it.

But for now, let's turn our attention to how to do it better. How can you be a boss who genuinely embodies power with boundaries, transparency, firmness, and fairness? How can you be a person who lives into the fullness of the power you have access to?

Inhabit Your Power

When I finished the rough draft of my dissertation, it was the middle of a broiling summer night in England. My fingers were stiff, my eyelids drooping. But finishing that first draft made me feel incredibly powerful. I had accomplished an important life goal. *I* was the person who had done it—no one else. I had developed the grit to stick with it. Years later, I still remember the sweetness of that moment. I knew I was someone who could stay with a massive project until the end. I felt the solidity of my body—the power of finishing. I was grateful, relieved, teary-eyed, and so present. It was a moment of quiet strength thrumming through me. This is an embodied memory of feeling my power.

While the experience of having power differs for everyone, here are some words and phrases that may help you feel your power. Feeling my power means:

- I am confident.

- I am certain.

- I am sure.

- Things will go my way.

- I can effect the change I want.

- I can bring what I want into the world.

- I can meet my needs.

- I have enough to share.

- I am abundant.

- I can access the people, learning, money, resources, and influence that I need.

- I feel relaxed and calm.

- I feel very rooted downward and connected upward, and solidly grounded in myself and my worth.

PRACTICE MOMENT: Feeling Your Power

Call to mind a time when you felt great personal power. Perhaps this was a time when you achieved an important goal or mastered a skill.

- What is the moment that comes to mind?

- What sensations and emotions were you experiencing?

- How did you know your power?

- How did you feel about it?

I call these "winning at life" moments. Sometimes they are boisterous and shiny. Sometimes they are solitary and private.

Notice how you feel when you feel powerful. How does your animal body feel powerful? It may feel like confidence or certainty. It may feel like solidity or being present. Maybe you feel your solid muscles or your strong spine. There are so many ways you can feel your power. Consider the following:

- How does your power show up in your body?

- How do you breathe?

- How do you move?

- Do you sit up straighter?
- What do you notice about being three-dimensional?

Once you've explored what your personal power feels like, see if you can put it into a few words or a simple phrase like those listed above. Then you'll have a simple litmus test to know if you are feeling your power or not.

Power Leaks

When you did your power assessment, did you notice any discrepancy between the power you hold and the power you feel?

I often forget to feel and notice the power I have. I slump, my breath gets shallow, and thoughts laced with self-doubt can creep in. Sometimes I forget how powerful I am.

Certain practices make you lose access to your power and impair your sense of leadership. These are not what you want to be practicing! They include:

- blaming—any time it's someone else's fault, you've moved your attention away from your own needs
- lack of accountability
- fighting with reality
- distracting yourself from what is
- denial
- minimizing
- dismissing
- acting out of alignment with your values
- assigning responsibility to someone else for your feelings

Most of these practices are unconscious, and we choose them to avoid discomfort. The problem is that they cost you a lot. When you engage in these practices, you give away your power.

While building your leadership capacity for discomfort, you'll start to notice when you choose these practices instead of being with your feelings and sensations. When you notice you're leaking power, you can lean into your embodiment practices to return to center. The rest of this chapter focuses on ways to reclaim your power, including when you start noticing those power leaks.

The Quick Power Fix

Part of your practice is remembering to lift up your chest and straighten your spine. When you do this, you reclaim responsibility for your own inner state. You act with agency, on your own behalf. Flex into your width and breathe a full breath into your center.

- Lift UP.
- Widen OUT.
- Breathe DEEP.

Up, out, and deep. It's that simple. It takes about three seconds. You can do it multiple times each day to connect with your power.

You can do great things when you connect with your body and embody your power! Your intuition is online again. Your decisions are more precise and more grounded.

The Power You Can Access but Haven't Earned

There is another critical aspect of power you need to learn to feel. You must discern between feeling the power you've earned (like my dissertation) and your privilege.

A few years ago, I was getting ready to have gender-affirming top surgery. I had spent months preparing: training hard at the gym, nourishing my body for optimal healing, and getting into the right headspace. My surgery was scheduled for a Monday morning. The Friday before, I received a call from my surgeon's office. They told me they hadn't received the results from my EKG and couldn't proceed without them. I needed to get my EKG results to the surgeon's office by the end of the day!

Unfortunately, no one had told me I needed to get an EKG. I didn't even know what an EKG was. I read over all my paperwork at least a dozen times, and there was no mention of an EKG. I called them back and asked them what an EKG was and where I needed to go to get one. Luckily, I was able to schedule a walk-in appointment for three p.m. that afternoon. All was well.

That afternoon, I went to San Francisco General Hospital for my EKG. I walked into a large rectangular waiting room filled with plastic chairs. The room was full of people who looked like they had been there for a while. The room was hot, and people were on their phones; one older man was asleep. There were probably thirty-five people in that room. I knew the office closed at four p.m. It's important to note that I was the only white-presenting person in the room.

There were two separate receptionist windows on opposite sides of the room. I walked to the first and presented my plastic card. The receptionist told me I did not have an appointment but to go to the second window and make one. I went to the second window, starting to panic for the second time that day. The receptionist at the second window was more helpful. She called my doctor's office before delivering the bad news. My appointment was actually at a completely different hospital on the other side of San Francisco! At that point it was 3:15 p.m., and rush-hour traffic meant it would take at least an hour to get to the correct hospital. And they would be closed.

At that moment, a large, white-appearing guy appeared behind the receptionist. He was a medical professional and asked what was going on. The receptionist told him, and he said not to worry; he would squeeze me in. He asked me to follow him back to a room where he performed my EKG and faxed the results to my doctor.

While this was happening, I was aware that I was getting preferential treatment. I believe it was because I am white. While thirty-five people of color sat in the waiting room, this man took care of me before the office closed for the weekend.

I felt bewildered. Because of white privilege, I had access to something that I needed. As a trans person, I needed that surgery not to be rescheduled. It was a complicated, intersectional situation. I took the privilege that was handed to me. It felt wrong but necessary at that moment. I knew I had not earned that power. I felt yucky inside as a white person but happy inside as a trans person. I could feel the difference between the unearned power of my white privilege and the earned power of something like completing my dissertation.

Sometimes you have access to power based on factors beyond your control, such as your gender or gender identity, skin color, who you know, or any of the multitude of factors that offer privilege.

How does this translate to you at work? It means you need to know what power you've earned feels like. You also need to understand how unearned power (privilege) feels different. One is yours; one is bestowed upon you. It's confusing, but it's important to try to feel the difference. It matters because how you hold the power you earn differs from how you hold privilege. Privilege can make you arrogant and entitled. The power you earn, when held well, does not do that. The power you acquire fairly will help you rest solidly in your certainty and your authority.

PRACTICE MOMENT: Feeling the Difference between Earned and Unearned Power

Recalling the previous exercise, call to mind the feelings and sensations you experienced in the moment when you felt your earned power. Notice in your body how that power feels.

Now let that go.

Next, call to mind an experience you had that resulted from your privilege, your unearned power. Was there a time when you received preferential treatment because of your identity, or when something was easier for you than it might have been for someone who did not share that identity?

Unearthing this memory might take some effort, especially if you've always had a lot of privilege, in which case having access to what you need feels normal to you.

Perhaps you were extended a line of credit you knew you didn't qualify for. Maybe you were let go with a warning after a traffic stop. Maybe you were given special attention by a salesperson even though there were other people waiting before you in the store.

Now feel into this sense of power. How does it feel different from earned power?

Can you put into words the differences you feel?

Try writing two lists:

Earned power feels like . . .

Unearned power feels like . . .

Discerning the Difference between Earned and Unearned Power

As a boss, knowing what your earned power is and what your unearned power is helps you empathize with your employees' access to power just for being who they are. Staying mindful and developing an analysis of these intersections between them and you will help you lead by using power-with. You must understand the power dynamics between you and each of your employees. If you pretend that power differentials based on identity aren't real, you cannot be a respectful leader.

Here's an example. Imagine you're a gay, forty-eight-year-old Black man from Haiti with a PhD in economics. You supervise a white, straight, twenty-nine-year-old cisgender woman with a BA from a state school who grew up in Massachusetts. The intersections of your identities and access to power are complex. Each of you inhabits various up-power and down-power positions. So who has more power? In this case, you do, at least while you're at work; but in a different context the power dynamic might shift. It's complicated, and there's no easy answer.

There is no right or wrong way to supervise based on identities. As with so many sources of potential conflict, effective communication is often the key to handling these issues with the care they need. Being able to talk about power in straightforward language keeps it from being minimized or downplayed. Get curious: be a boss who seeks to understand how your dragon tail affects your employees.

Once you can feel the difference between your earned and unearned power, you can make decisions based on that understanding. For example, let's say you're a white man and you understand how unearned power enables those who have it to speak first. As part of your leadership, you adopt a practice of asking white men to hold off on speaking first in meetings. Or perhaps you are cisgender, and some folks on your team are fussing about the new company policy requiring them to put their pronouns in their email tagline. You realize that as a cis person, you can speak up about why including pronouns is important.

Another example could be that when someone you supervise who has less access to unearned power comes to your office to tell you about a negative experience they're having, you listen closely and thank them for their bravery in offering you feedback. Again, unearned power is not bad in and of itself. Used wisely, it can help build inclusive and diverse teams that thrive.

Once I could feel my power as the boss, I could accept the truth that leaders are held to a higher standard of conduct. As I'm sure you know, it's in the fine print of your unwritten contract: you are supposed to model ethical behavior. Part of the exchange of people accepting your leadership means they get to turn to you for embodied guidance. As a boss, you are always coaching, mentoring, and teaching. That means using your power, both earned and unearned, to lift up those you supervise. And here you thought you were just running a company!

As a boss, you must be in your integrity. When you inadvertently fail at this because you are human, you have to own up to it. Part of your dragon tail includes being someone people look up to.

Here is an example of what can happen after you embody your power and inhabit your leadership. One of my employees came to me about a year into our working relationship. They told me they needed to take some time off for personal reasons at a very intense part of our work cycle. This particular person was reserved and contained. They had very professional boundaries. Their work was always precise and dependable.

When they came to me, something in their body language read as emotional distress. My gut told me something was wrong. I could have ignored it, but I chose to ask about it instead, in a way that left them plenty of room to decline. Instead, they opened up. They told me about a personal situation that gravely affected their safety and well-being.

I leveraged the power at my disposal to reassign that person's obligations. We hired an outside freelancer to take on part of the project. We gave them the time and space they needed to take care of themselves. The team rallied around them with messages of care and support. In my bones, I felt the rightness of this course of action. It cost the company more in the short term but protected a valuable employee in the long term. And the situation concluded with me feeling I had acted fully in my integrity and had wielded my earned power well.

Talking about Power at Work

People want power so they can meet their needs and satisfy their desires. Unfortunately, many of us have been taught to compete for power. Dr. Greg Barnett, senior vice president of science for the Predictive Index, expresses the conventional wisdom that power involves competition: "Team power dynamics represent the reality that with any team or group of people, there's a finite amount of power available to get things done and make things happen according to one's agenda. In that way, power is really a resource people have to compete for. They compete for it in very different ways. Some people use charisma and charm, others are more forceful and assertive, while still others use facts and figures to wrestle power back."

While a degree of playful competition may serve a team whose members enjoy that, it can also create an environment of mistrust. If you want to create an atmosphere of collaboration, normalize talking about power dynamics. For many, this breaks a social taboo; yet it is necessary. One of the crucial questions a team must address is: how do we distribute power? This question is always answered, but rarely is it handled with transparency.

So how do you talk about power at work?

Everyone you manage will have a different experience of the power dynamics occurring on the team. Individuals have varying levels of access to formal and informal power. People are more or less confident, have earned a higher or lower degree of trust and respect from the group, and have different levels of access to their own agency. Even as you try to create a team where power is openly discussed and power is shared, there is no team where everyone has the same level of influence forever.

The principle of naming what is comes in super handy here. Before you can name what is, you need to observe, and then describe the behaviors you're noticing. This is similar to how you practice observing in your body, and using words to describe your experience.

Observation means resting back in yourself and taking a break from meaning-making. From your back body, what do you notice about an interaction between two employees? What are their words, and what are their actions?

Pro tip: the skill of observation separate from analysis is easy to practice. Next time you're watching two people interact, or watching a film with characters interacting, see if you can name just their words and actions, minus all the fascinating stories your brain makes up. Just the facts!

Power dynamics are invisible, but deeply felt, like the wind. Develop your superpower for noticing people's words and actions. Then, using words, you can gently inquire about their inner experience.

For example, Jill leads a team of three stonemasons. Her company is known for inspired, creative, and meticulous residential landscaping. Recently, Jill noticed that two of her employees seemed very close, while the third, Matt, often worked alone. He was also the newest to join the team. Jill noticed that the quality of his work had decreased over the last two months, and she was concerned. Jill asked him for a meeting so she could hear about what was going on. Here's their conversation, with Jill first observing and naming, and then extending curiosity.

Jill: Thanks for meeting with me, Matt. I wanted to take some time to check in with you and see how being on the team is feeling.

Matt: It's okay, I'm feeling good about things.

Jill: Okay to share what I'm observing? [obtaining consent]

Matt: Sure.

Jill: When I see you working with the others, I often notice you working by yourself, while they work together. [making observation] Have you noticed that?

Matt: Yeah, but it's okay.

Jill: Well, I'm curious if you feel supported coming onto the team. [extending an opening for Matt to share how he feels]

Matt: Yeah, I don't know, it's okay.

Jill: [sensing Matt's reluctance to make waves] I don't know if my guess is true, but it kind of looks like the others are teaming up. I can imagine it might be helpful for you to feel more a part of the team. Does that sound right?

Matt: Yes, but I'm not sure how.

Jill: Thanks for telling me. I know they have worked together for a long time. [acknowledging experiential power] My gut tells me we need to sort this out. I'm going to talk with them as well, without mentioning our conversation. I want you to feel welcome and supported.

Matt: That would be great, but I don't want them to think I said anything. [expressing concern about retaliation]

Jill: Totally. I'll make sure it's coming from me. It's important to me that we have a team that's working together and taking care of everybody. Let's meet again in two weeks and see if anything feels different for you.

In this example, Jill is using her observations and her words to create an opening where she and Matt can talk more freely. She senses his awareness of the power dynamics, both with her and with the other employees. She's sensitive to his concerns, wants to protect a valuable employee, and wants to create cohesion and harmony on the team. She finds a strategy to address her concerns without resorting to power-over (i.e., shaming Matt for poor work or her other employees for not including Matt).

You notice that she tracks the power dynamics through words and actions. Although explicit discussion of power dynamics can sometimes be useful, it is also helpful to be sensitive to how hard it is for most people to talk about power directly.

Tips for Using Power-With

- Create a written list of clearly defined shared goals, so everyone can get behind them.

- Practice consent at work. How your employees feel matters. (We'll discuss consent much more in chapter 9.)

- Normalize saying and hearing no within your team.

- Have written, clearly defined roles and responsibilities. Keep those job descriptions updated! Ask your team members to update their job descriptions as part of your review process. They are likely doing things you aren't aware of that were not in their original contract. Update their pay accordingly.

- Understand the needs of each individual. Introverts and extroverts have different needs on a team.

- During meetings, have a stopwatch, and time people's shares so that all voices get equal opportunities to be heard. Go around in a circle to make sure everyone has a chance to speak, not just the loudest and first voices. People can pass if they want to.

- Find communication strategies that honor everyone's needs. People have different preferences. Some prefer meetings; others prefer email or platforms like Slack. Have communication guidelines that manage expectations for how and when people will respond. These can be created within your team.

- Invite in your own and your employees' felt-sense wisdom. This sounds like, "What does your gut say about that?" or "Anybody notice anything in their bodies about how we should move forward?"

- State over and over that you want to hear their feedback, their yeses and nos. When they give it to you, receive it with gratitude. This builds trust in your ability to show up for honest feedback.

- Provide opportunities for staff to build experiential power by offering mentorship or affinity groups.

- Share relational power by not playing favorites and treating team members with care and curiosity.

- When you recognize that someone on your team has less access to any kind of power, you can lift them up.

- Recognize that doing the work around recognizing your power and power dynamics is a lifelong process, since power is always in flux.

Chapter 5 Takeaways

O You may have access to power you cannot yet feel. You have to learn how to feel your power to use it effectively.

O Power includes your ability to influence others. Power is having a choice about how you respond to situations. It also includes your internal and external access to the resources required to meet your needs.

O Some power you earn; some you have as a result of social privilege. You can learn to tell the difference between them. This helps you use your access to power with integrity.

O You can normalize talking about power at work. It breaks a social taboo to talk about power.

O Separating observations from analysis opens a path to speaking about power.

6

EMBODYING YOUR LEADERSHIP

Embodied Leadership Presence and Practices

Your power as a leader comes from your embodied presence. You are powerful because you can tap into your body wisdom, your wealth of experience, and your trained capacities.

Becoming a leader is a practice that takes a lifetime. It's essential to develop a growth mindset that allows you to always be learning and training, developing new muscles of leadership, and getting in touch with more and more body intelligence. You already know you can't think your way into being a better leader. Practicing—and especially practicing while on the job—is key.

PRACTICE MOMENT: Developing Your Leader Body

For this exercise, you'll do some writing.

Call to mind your embodied role model. What about them makes their leadership valuable? What words would you use to describe them?

Now consider how you want to be a leader. Make a list of at least ten words you want to embody in your leadership. These can be leadership traits, like "integrity" or "power from within." They can also describe your leadership body, like "graceful" or "contained." Paint a picture in words of who you want to be as a leader, what you want to curate, what you want to cultivate.

Now add to your list how your body as a leader feels. This can be expressed in words like "ease" or "confident."

Who you are as a leader is a combination of how you are and how you feel. You are your actions, plus your internal felt sense. Who do you want to be? Or, who are you already that emerges as you practice?

This visioning exercise gives you a chance to think about who you want to be as you embody leadership. It also lets you think about how you'll feel when you're there. I'm guessing that how you want to feel is a huge part of why you're changing. You want to feel more at ease and be less stressed.

For change to stick, it has to happen in your body. You determine your course by deciding who you want to be and why it matters to be that way.

Once you know who you want to be as a leader and why, you can determine the most beneficial practices for yourself. Practice is the fast track to getting where you want to be. The capacities and skills you want to have can all be developed through deliberate, focused practice, which often requires much less effort than you would think. Small amounts of conscious practice can get you there.

You can make up your own practices based on your unique needs. There's no single approach that works for everyone. Rather, you determine the approach based on the exact skill or capacity you want.

For example, let's say you want to be more present. Trying to "be more present" often leads to feelings of frustration and confusion because the endeavor is phrased in vague, nonspecific terms, and the actual action you're supposed to take is unclear. You don't practice "being more present."

Instead, you come up with a concrete practice that gives the *result* of more presence. So for this skill, you might choose a simple shift to widen your vision to take in the periphery while breathing. Then, as you do that, you notice you are straining your muscles around your eyes. So you respond by breathing ease into your eye muscles. You then notice that you're sitting forward. You get curious about what would happen if you sat back. When you sit back, you notice that your diaphragm is tight, so you breathe into your belly. Then you realize you're thirsty, so you drink some water. Congratulations—you have just become more present! This is somatic practice at work. You paid attention to your body and responded wisely.

The benefits of a practice become evident over time. Self-mastery is the process of becoming skilled in the areas you desire. You practice what and where it matters. It follows that if you want to be better at a work-related skill, it's most effective to practice in your workplace.

For example, being a present leader matters to me. I've long had a practice of saying good morning to my team in a tone that conveys care. Part of my leadership is to welcome them to work each morning. It requires me to remember what I value and be present when I see them. It requires me to ground and speak from an embodied place.

Deciding to practice something new is an investigation. You don't know how that practice will feel, or what the result will be. You don't even know if it will be the right practice. That's why the tone of curiosity and non-judgment is so important. So many times we embark on a new practice and then drop it and feel like failures. But as a leader, that tired old story doesn't serve you. This is where a growth mindset comes in. Always be learning.

Choose a practice and notice what happens. Don't commit to that practice until you have ascertained that it is the proper practice and it helps you. Approach this exploration with a sense of openness, and let go of any rigidity you may have about doing it "the right way."

PRACTICE MOMENT: Embodying Your Leadership

This practice is a bit longer. Try giving yourself fifteen minutes or more when you can be quiet and uninterrupted.

Revisit the list of competencies from chapter 2 (on page 29) that you need as a leader.

As a leader, you need to be able to do the following:

- be present
- collaborate
- listen
- repair conflict
- trust and be trusted
- observe and name what is
- be curious
- envision
- inspire
- discern aligned action
- set boundaries
- decide
- take action
- receive support
- be with discomfort

On this list, what excites you? Choose a capacity to develop a practice around.

Make note of the capacity you want to build.

What is one minor action you could perform or step you could take toward having that capacity?

For example, if you chose "set boundaries," what is one boundary you could set right now? Either with yourself or another? Start small; don't go for the biggest thing right off the bat.

Maybe you set this boundary: "I will take a break from work and eat my lunch today." Set that boundary and then notice how you feel. During or after this practice, try on a new narrative like, "I have boundaries with work."

If you chose "take action," what is one small action you can take right now? Can you send an email you've been procrastinating on? Pay a bill? Clean up a mess? Do it, and while you're doing it, try saying, "I am someone who takes action." Notice what happens.

If you chose "trust," can you take one breath and, on your exhale, practice trusting a particular team member or situation? Maybe you speak the phrase, "I am trusting this moment." Go ahead and do your practice and collect data on the result. What happened?

Practice does not have to be a big formal structure, although it can be. As you train your body to be a leader's body, you take small, incremental steps that help you build to higher capacities. Practice is how you create lasting somatic transformation. Practice will get you where you want to be if you can be patient. Need to train patience? What's a good practice for that?

Remember: change = new narrative + why it matters + new practice/s + new way to be/live/feel/move in your body.

Now that you know the capacity you want to expand, the practice you want to do, and the new narrative you wish to embody, let's put it all together.

I suggest standing for this practice, if you can. Otherwise, sitting will work.

First, take several minutes to B.B.O.D.Y. (return to chapter 4 if you need a refresher).

Once you feel present and embodied, do whatever practice you have chosen, feel your power, and name your new narrative to yourself.

Now imagine yourself receiving some negative impact from work: an unpleasant email or feedback from an unhappy employee.

Notice how this affects your groundedness. Do you lose center or fall off your practice?

Now move back into your practice. From this place of grounded, centered leadership, feel how to respond to the impact.

When you feel complete, finish the practice and celebrate. You have successfully embodied leadership. Look at that dragon tail sparkle in the sun!

Ten Steps to Change

1. Choose a new capacity, and create the narrative you want to embody. Back in chapter 1, you explored your current narratives and the narratives you would like to embody. What is the new story you're practicing?

2. Decide why it matters to you.

3. Consider how you'll know you have embodied this capacity. What will it feel like?

4. Think of a small action you can take that moves you toward what you want.

5. Do it, and while you do it, say your new narrative or your "why" to yourself.

6. Celebrate whenever you do your practice.

7. Reflect. How do you feel now? Your reflection can be directly after the practice, or after some interval of practice.

8. Repeat as needed, at the right level of effort and frequency for you.

9. Adjust your practice to respond to your needs.

10. Repeat until integrated.

Let's look at the ten steps to change in action by discussing the case of Kai, a product design lead for a company producing digital educational materials.

1. Kai wants to develop his capacity to inspire his team. The new narrative he crafts is, "I am a leader who inspires creativity."

2. Inspiring others matters to Kai because he wants to build a team culture of risk and innovation.

3. Kai feels he will have embodied this new capacity and narrative when he sees members of his team bringing up cool, expansive ideas during the planning phase—ideas that might not ever work.

4. Kai decides to research the qualities of inspirational leaders. He makes a list of leaders he has had who have inspired him, and he looks at their common traits. He finds that he is most inspired by ethical behavior, when words, values, and actions all align. He creates a document that states his values, and he posts it in his office. He talks about it with his team, and he tells them his intention is to live aligned with these values and he is open to feedback.

5. He reads his list out loud every day when starting work. Kai reminds himself frequently that he's building the capacity to inspire others.

6. After he reads his list, Kai celebrates by checking it off his daily to-do list, starting his day with an accomplishment.

7. As he implements this new practice, Kai checks in about how he feels on a somewhat regular basis. He asks himself what he notices about aligning his values and his actions. Does he feel inspiring?

8. In the beginning, Kai does his practice daily.

9. As he builds capacity for inspiring others, he adds a practice of telling his team whenever he feels he's fallen short of one of those values. He normalizes making mistakes and using them as growth opportunities. After a couple of months, Kai finds

that he no longer needs to read his values aloud. He knows them by heart.

10. The new capacity is integrated. Kai sees his team taking new creative risks, and he celebrates the culture he has supported.

The Easiest Way to Fail at a Practice

While building a practice can be relatively simple, there are plenty of ways you can get in your own way and sabotage your success. Here are a few of the most common ways you can set yourself up for failure:

- **Committing to a frequency and duration that don't align with your life.** For example, "I will practice this every day for two hours." Where are you getting those two hours? Trying to force too rigid a structure early in your practice usually leads to you stopping the practice because the logistics don't work.

- **Not getting extra support during transitions.** Most people fall off their practices during transition times: vacation, illness, family visiting. All of life's minor changes that shift your routine are transitions.

- **Being hard on yourself.** If you wouldn't say it to a child you're coaching, don't say it to yourself.

- **Getting into power struggles with your resistance.** Forget it. Your resistance is stronger. It will always win. Instead, you have to enlist it as an ally.

- **Not dating a practice before you marry it.** Gather data first. See if that practice is useful before making a commitment to it.

- **Being rigid in your thinking;** that is, "This is the only way to accomplish my goal."

- **Forgetting that getting back up after falling down is always part of the practice.** You will miss days, weeks, or maybe even years of your practice. It's not the end if it's the right practice. Get back up and start practicing again.

- **Forgetting that behavioral change needs lots of structure and support.**

- **Forgetting to tend to the part of you that is scared.** Change is scary; it's the end of an older way of being. You seldom have an internal consensus for change. Some part of you is tenaciously holding on to how things were for a good reason. You've got to be tender with that part and ask what it needs to get on board. Remember to always be gentle and kind with yourself.

In this chapter, you're learning how to practice somatic awareness at work, which facilitates a powerful leadership quality: presence. Here's a story about a client learning to feel himself at work.

Feeling Yourself Inside Yourself: Meet Finn

Finn was a client who was in upper management in a Silicon Valley tech firm. He had risen to leadership quickly, but he was miserable at work. Not coincidentally, he felt trapped in his marriage. Although he had financial and career success, he was deeply unhappy.

When he arrived in my office, his body spoke worlds about him. Finn was tall, classically handsome, well dressed, and athletic. But as a somatic coach trained in making assessments, I noticed his motions were tight and rigid. He barely moved during our session, and I couldn't see his chest rising and falling with his breath. His stomach looked contracted. When I sat with him, it felt like there was no room for him in his own life. He was enduring life, not enjoying it. He told me what he wanted more than anything was to feel connected with the spirituality he had experienced as a young man.

We decided he would use his workplace to practice embodiment. He would practice feeling himself at work. It's essential to train the skills you want to develop in the environment in which you want them to appear, and Finn wanted to feel more connected with his creativity at work.

He started to take two five-minute embodiment breaks each day. He set the alarm on his phone so he wouldn't forget. When the alarm went off, he would stand up in his office and do the B.B.O.D.Y. practice.

Remembering to breathe was the most challenging part for him, and he wasn't immediately successful. This frustrated him because he was successful in so many areas of his life.

Part of my job as a somatic coach is to help clients bridge that terrible middle bit, when you've set a course for a new somatic body but you haven't arrived there yet. In the middle of the change process, your resolve, commitment, and even memory of why you're doing this are tested. I help the client hold the vision for where they can get if they stick with it through this frustrating terrain. I wasn't sure Finn would stick with it, but he did. He dug in deeper, determined to figure out how to feel connected with himself.

We developed and tested more somatic practices he could use at work. He loved to walk in his neighborhood, and he started to practice noticing his legs as he walked. Gradually, he reported that he was feeling less blocked in his career. Over the weeks and months that followed, he eventually learned to breathe more fully. In his words, he learned to "feel me inside of myself."

He allowed his team to support him, and they were doing better work than they had previously. There were moments in our sessions when his smile reached his eyes. When we completed our work, he had taken on a new role at work that involved a lot more creativity. His team was giving him positive feedback. He had brought out his paints at home and was working on creating an oracle deck. He felt connected to Spirit. It took some time, but with practice, he could feel himself more. The difference was palpable not just to him but also to those he worked with.

Presence

The capacity to be present is essential for a leader. But what does it mean? And how do you do it? You're present when you are right here, right now, in this moment, dwelling in your current existence. Presence is the ability to direct your attention to what is in front of you at the moment. When you think about your embodied role model, what do you notice about their level of presence?

I have a morning meditation practice. After I wake, I head to my meditation cushion, light a candle, and sit my butt down. Even though I'm barely awake, my thoughts are already moving quickly. I have an intention to sit and be present, but every morning, I forget my intention. I sit there thinking about what will happen in my day. I think about what I have to do and the conversations I need to have. Random bits of dreams or worries make their way into my brain. After five or ten minutes of this, I realize I'm not present. I use the B.B.O.D.Y. practice and wrangle my attention back to what is happening. I am sitting on a cushion. I have a body. I am breathing.

Spending a few minutes being with myself is an accomplishment, every day. Being and feeling in the here and now is not always easy. When someone is fully present with you, though, you feel it. When you receive the full benefit of someone's attention, your system feels met.

Embodiment is a partnership between your body and your mind. It's when you direct your attention toward feeling, when you allow yourself to be here and now. Embodiment requires your presence.

As a leader, your capacity for being present is crucial. You need to know how to direct your ten thousand to-do thoughts. You need to be able to push the pause button and show up. Being present with someone is how you honor their personhood. If you cannot be present with yourself, it will be challenging to be present with others.

PRACTICE MOMENT: Get Present

In this practice, you'll bring your attention to right here and right now. You'll need a glass of water or another beverage.

First, take a few minutes to B.B.O.D.Y.

Once you can feel yourself inside yourself, spend a minute or two taking in your surroundings. Your senses will help.

What do you see? Allow your eyes to go where they want to go.

What do you smell? Are there any scents you notice now that were in the background before?

What sounds do you hear?

What does your body feel? Are you sitting? Which parts of you are in contact with a surface?

Now sip your beverage, paying attention to how the liquid feels in your mouth and moves down your throat.

When you get distracted, return your awareness to the here and now.

Once you feel present and situated in time and space, acknowledge that this is what "present" feels like today.

Somatic Awareness Rituals at Work

Becoming somatically aware at work takes time and practice. Sometimes you'll nail it; other times, you'll forget to feel yourself for hours, days, or weeks at a time. Growth is often not a linear process, and it is never a straight line. Forgetting and remembering are normal parts of the embodiment process. Sustained change requires practice.

Building rituals can help. This doesn't necessarily mean something religious or spiritual, although it can, if that aligns with your beliefs. Rituals are any habits you do with intention, and so much of embodiment is about making new, intentional habits for yourself. For example, before I sit down to work, I have a series of things I do. I get a glass of water. I spray my plants. I light a candle, and then I put on the same piece of music I start every work session with. I take a belly breath and feel my feet on the floor. These actions trigger my brain into knowing that it is work time now.

Developing a practice of B.B.O.D.Y. before entering important conversations and meetings will help you feel connected with yourself. You'll have quicker access to necessary gut-check information, you'll be able to feel when something is off, and your somatic awareness will guide you toward the correct paths of action.

You can easily build B.B.O.D.Y. breaks into your day. For instance, I have a chime on my phone that rings every hour to remind me to do them. If you're in a rush, you can B.B.O.D.Y in less than thirty seconds—and a little goes a long way. Ironically, the smallest amount of conscious practice can create a considerable positive impact. These minor changes add up. In addition, if you notice you're feeling a physical need during your day, such as hunger, thirst, or the need to use the bathroom, take action to meet that need ASAP. Tending to your needs when you have them builds body trust and helps you remember to check in with yourself.

Those moments when stressful impact hits you are when you need your practice the most. That's also when you're least likely to remember to do it or want to do it. Conflict, upsetting emails, difficult conversations—these are all times when feeling your body can support you. Once you establish a body trust relationship, your body can be your haven. It's the resource you always have access to.

PRACTICE MOMENT: Embodiment Rituals

What embodiment rituals do you want to set up for yourself at key points during your day? Take some time now to write down your somatic awareness plan for work. Beginnings, endings, and other transitions are important, so I suggest you include a ritual for the start and finish of your day. Consider the following as you write up your embodiment ritual plan:

- What is your intention? "I practice feeling myself at work" is a good one.

- At what times or in which situations will you practice embodiment rituals at work?

- How will you begin your somatic practice? Do you take a breath, feel your feet, settle on your frame, or . . .?

- What practice will you do? Will you B.B.O.D.Y? Do some yoga? Something else?

- How will you close your day with somatic practice so you feel complete?

You have done deep work to decide what kind of boss you want to be, how to responsibly access your power, and how to develop practices to align your words and actions. The next chapter discusses how to create a workplace culture that aligns with your values, acknowledging that most people have trauma.

We'll discuss the importance of creating a trauma-informed workplace, but that doesn't mean we should neglect nurturing a workplace that also honors joy and pleasure. Creating a workplace that values embodiment means valuing the whole spectrum of human experience.

Chapter 6 Takeaways

O Establish habits and rituals, and work to practice embodiment.

O Practice a new skill in the place where you want to use it.

O Change is a process you can design.

O You need to B.B.O.D.Y. the most when life is the most difficult, such as when you receive stressful impact at work.

7

TRAUMA AND TRIGGERS

ACCORDING TO THE NATIONAL COUNCIL for Behavioral Health, 70 percent of American adults have experienced some type of traumatic event at least once in their lives. People often think of trauma in terms of war, abuse, or assault, but trauma can also deeply affect the workplace, both through harmful events that occur there and through the histories your employees bring with them.

Being an embodied boss includes creating a trauma-informed workplace. The collective traumas caused by COVID-19, increased racial and economic injustice, climate change, and growing global instability are the water we swim in, affecting us all. Who we are in our lives is who we are at work, so if you have trauma in your life, there is a 100 percent chance it will show up on the job. And making space for trauma at work is antithetical to the capitalist value of profit over people. That's why creating space for both your and your employees' whole selves matters now more than ever.

For example, Nora, an employee of mine, went through a period when she missed several weekly team meetings and deadlines. She was usually very present, competent, and responsible, so this was out of character for her. After a few weeks of this behavior, we had a conversation. I learned that she was going through a horrific divorce and that her grandmother was hospitalized for COVID and likely wouldn't pull through. She also told me she had lost her mom at a very young age, and her grandmother had raised her and had been the only constant in her life. Nora said she hadn't wanted to tell me because she worried I would think she wasn't doing a good job of keeping her home life separate from work. She worried about losing her job, especially if she couldn't maintain her performance.

You've probably heard similar stories from people you manage. The human part of me understood that she couldn't focus on her work right now and that trauma was at play. But I also felt frustrated because, as the boss, I needed Nora's work to get done. We worked through it and came up with a plan, but I name this here to say that being a trauma-informed workplace means confronting the tension between people and profitability. And you will likely feel that tension in your body.

However, compartmentalization contradicts what you're trying to do, both for yourself and for your employees. You cannot be embodied if you live your life in pieces, and neither can your employees. You are who you are, both at work and at home, and so are they. They bring their whole selves to work with them, as do you.

This is not to say that a trauma-informed workplace should coddle people. Professionalism is still essential. When you understand trauma, you can respond with compassion and care while still maintaining a professional work environment.

What Is Trauma?

Trauma occurs when a person is overwhelmed by events or circumstances and responds with intense fear, horror, and helplessness. Extreme stress overwhelms the person's capacity to cope. Trauma is also subjective: what one person finds traumatic, another person may shake off.

Common causes of trauma include:

- childhood abuse or neglect
- witnessing acts of violence
- medical interventions
- grief and loss

- cultural, intergenerational, and historical trauma
- physical, emotional, or sexual abuse
- accidents and natural disasters
- war

When your brain perceives a threat, your body automatically prepares to take action. This is the survival instinct at work, when your nervous system jumps into fight or flight mode. Ideally, you either win the fight or run away to safety, and the survival response is completed.

But what happens if you can't respond—or can't respond without making a significant trade-off? Someone yells "Run!" as a swarm of angry bees flies toward you, but the only place to run is into a river swarming with hungry alligators. You can't fight the bees, and you can't run away. There are no safe options. You do nothing, caught in the moment. You freeze.

When you can't or don't take action on your own behalf, the survival response is incomplete, according to Peter Levine's trauma research. When you can't complete the survival response, trauma can occur. Even if you physically survive the experience, some part of you gets stuck at that moment. These incomplete survival responses get stored in the tissues of your body as trauma.

Sometimes you have to make a trade-off to survive. Maybe you survive the bees by crouching down low and only submerging your legs in the river. Some bees sting you, but not enough to kill you, and the alligators mutilate your legs, but the rest of you survives. People who find themselves in overwhelming situations have to make trade-offs all the time.

Trade-offs involve offering up a part of yourself to ensure survival. This isn't usually a body part, like in the case of the alligators; more often it's something else that matters to you. Perhaps you try to appease the person or the situation causing the threat (this is sometimes referred to as the "fawn" response). Maybe you act like it's okay when it's not.

Even though you survived the experience with the bees and the alligators, for the rest of your life you'll freeze and start to panic whenever you see a bee. The trauma is still with you. It causes you to respond to something in the past as if it's happening in the present. Trauma is a physical wound in the body that prohibits spontaneous action. It's also a wound in the mind that, when unresolved, keeps people trapped in time. The impact of trauma exists long after the traumatic event, affecting relationships, capacities, and communities.

What Is a Trigger?

Triggers are essentially traumatic body memories. They're unprocessed information in your tissues and nervous system. When you're triggered, your body remembers a past threat and applies it to a current situation, experiencing a set of sensations and emotions that are not within your control. You are no longer in the present moment; you are instead responding to something from your past. Triggers are from the past, but they don't know it. They act like they're in the present. They do everything possible to convince you that the original cause of the trauma is taking place now. They tell you that you can't handle what's happening. Their most insidious quality is the self-doubt they induce. Your triggers allow you to see the trauma you hold that is not yet fully processed.

Being triggered can look something like this: your partner gets angry and raises their voice, and you suddenly feel tiny. You pull inward. You're unable to speak. Your system is responding like it did when you were a kid. Adult-you knows there's nothing to fear from your partner, but kid-you is freaking out, worried you are about to get hit. Your system is triggered by a memory of an angry parent who lashed out.

Triggers are that moment when someone says something to you, and you feel the bottom drop out of your stomach. Or you feel the terrible flush of mortification. You're suddenly filled with dread, rage, and terror. Emotions that often indicate triggers are fear, anger, betrayal, and abandonment. Sensations that indicate triggers include feeling that things are moving fast inside, or feeling like you're spinning or dropping. You lose your center. You lose your feeling of groundedness. You lose access to calm. It can feel like you've lost control, like someone else is driving you.

But sometimes it's hard to know when you're triggered. Recognizing it is half the battle. A key indication that you're triggered is when you notice that your reaction is more significant than the current situation calls for, or when there is a sudden and seemingly inexplicable change in your feelings. But even when you notice you're triggered, it can be hard to admit it. Many people find it nearly impossible to communicate when they're caught in a trauma response.

When you're triggered, your survival strategies kick in because your body is perceiving a past threat in a current situation. You immediately react to the situation or person with whatever go-to strategy is stored in your body, either moving toward, moving away from, or moving against—fight, flight, freeze, dissociate, appease, collapse. In a triggered state, you don't choose your strategies. They just happen, and they happen too quickly and automatically for you to respond with your embodied, fully conscious self.

It's important to understand that while we each have all possible survival strategies, in our past some worked out for us better than others. For example, if a little kid learns that by running away he avoids physical punishment, but if he stays and fights he gets hit, his flight response is more effective in helping him to survive. This means that over time, the flight response becomes a stronger neural pathway.

As a boss, you need to know what somatic survival response you trend toward. This is because our survival responses have an impact on those around us. If you're a boss who has a flight response to conflict, when you're triggered your employees will be left hanging as you disappear. If you have a fight response, your employees may be on the receiving end of some unskillful use of power as your anger dominates the meeting.

Knowing your survival responses allows you to communicate ahead of time. If you know you typically respond by fighting, then you can tell your employees, "Hey, when I get triggered I get angry. If I get triggered I'll try to take myself out of the situation and return when I'm calm, but I just want you to know." Communicating about survival responses allows others to understand you better, reduces shame about the response, and acknowledges your own humanity. Knowledge is power, and by knowing your responses, you can take care of yourself and your team.

Basic Information about Triggers

- Triggers are body memories of a time when your system was overwhelmed.

- Your body remembers the past threat and applies it to a current situation.

- You are no longer in the present moment but responding to something from your past.

- Triggers are accompanied by a somatic response—fight, flight, freeze, appease, collapse, or dissociate—initiating in your amygdala.

- Triggers hijack your amygdala and take your neocortex offline.

- It is almost impossible to make grounded decisions when triggered.

- You can complete the trigger response to avoid causing more trauma.

Wouldn't It Be Better If I Didn't Get Triggered Anymore?

Many of my clients hope that by doing somatic work, they will no longer be triggered. It does help to explore your triggers and bring compassion and healing to what lies beneath them, but your triggers have become wired into your nervous system. They are vital information your brain perceives with the intention of helping you survive. Triggers will lessen over time when explored in this manner, but they do not disappear. Lessening means they will occur less frequently, with less intensity, and you may have more choice in the moment. Accept that you will get triggered, and it is your responsibility to deal with it. This is not to say you have no choice in the matter and are forever at the mercy of your triggers. Your nervous system is resilient and can develop new neural pathways, a property called neuroplasticity. This means your nervous system can grow and change and develop new responses over time.

Many people try not to get triggered or to pretend they're not triggered. However, your life becomes very small if you try to avoid being triggered. It's more effective to learn how to be with yourself with kindness and compassion when you're triggered.

If you slow down, you can access more options. Viktor Frankl said, "Between stimulus and response there is a space. In that space is our power to choose our response. In our response lies our growth and our freedom." We don't have any choice about what our triggers are, but we can choose how we deal with them. Triggers often feel like time is speeding up, which can create a sense of urgency. Although slowing down in such situations is counterintuitive, it's the right thing to do because it allows you to choose from a centered and grounded place.

Four Steps to Deal with Triggers: Respond, Don't React

1. **Acknowledge that you're triggered.** Your nervous system is elevated. You feel heightened intensity of sensation and emotion.

2. **Take a break.** This might mean leaving the space you're in, going for a walk, taking a trip to the bathroom, or watching cat videos on the socials. Give yourself and your system time to calm down, with no pressure to make any decisions.

3. **Get into your body.** B.B.O.D.Y./return to center/resource yourself. Have a snack; move around.

4. **Choose how to deal with the situation.** You may need to get support first in order to suss out more options. This is the point when you respond to the situation. You've named it, taken time, and gotten into your body, and now you're ready to consider how to respond to your own needs and the situation.

"How" Matters Most

You'll have to navigate your own triggers at work, as well as those of your employees. It's unavoidable. This may sound daunting, but you can develop skills for working with triggers. One way to think about triggers is that they are loud, unmet needs. *How* you are with yourself and others matters. Kindness matters most.

If a little kid is freaking out about something scary, you don't yell at them for feeling afraid. You treat them gently and tenderly. This is how you want to be with yourself, too. Extending care to yourself when you're having a hard time is the most helpful thing you can do.

Triggers try to define the way things are in your life. They can make you afraid and doubt yourself. Have you ever thought, "Well, that triggers me, so I guess I can't do that anymore"? Triggers like to tell you that you cannot handle certain situations. This is a residual overwhelm. But know that your triggers are not bigger or stronger than you. You can learn to work with them.

Do you remember Stan, my client who didn't want intimacy with his partner but forced himself to be intimate anyway? His body shut down because he was overriding his trigger. He had to learn to be gentle with himself and care for that part of him that was afraid. When he didn't push through but responded to himself kindly, he became able to work with the trigger differently.

People get triggered at work All. The. Time. You probably do too. Someone mentions your old boss's name, and you feel your throat lock up and your stomach clench. One of my "favorite" triggers is when a boss says, "I need to talk to you."

Of course you don't want to be triggered. Being triggered and reactive sucks because it takes you away from center, and you lose control of yourself. You behave in ways you regret. Wouldn't it be great if people would just act right and not trigger you?

Here's a hard thing about triggers, particularly in the workplace: they can make you display controlling tendencies. You want to control other people's behavior so they don't do things that upset you. This is an understandable response, but it doesn't lend itself to creating a healthy workplace.

Maybe employees will comply with your demands in the short term, but in the long term you'll pay the price for your controlling behavior.

Life gets smaller when you try to never be triggered. You'll learn to tolerate less and less—the opposite of building capacity. The path to greater freedom is to learn to *work with* your triggers, not to avoid them. Rather than trying to prevent them from ever occurring again, you face them with courage, and you become resilient.

When you're triggered, it's easy to forget all the amazing resources you have, all the skills you've built, and all the practice you have under your belt. But your triggers are yours, and you can learn to be responsible for them. It's your responsibility to find more adult and compassionate ways of being with yourself.

Triggers are often signs of something not yet grieved, signaling a loss or harm of some kind that has not been processed or healed. At the root of a trigger, you'll often find something that needs to be mourned. When you're triggered, it's common to immediately blame the person who "triggered" you. But here's another option: next time you are triggered and feeling blamey, ask yourself, "What do I need?"

The Co-trigger

When you're triggered, you can't find common ground with others. And you know what else? Triggers are contagious! Your employee comes to you, triggered about something, and the next thing you know, you're triggered too. If you've ever been in a relationship, you know what I mean.

The co-trigger is the quintessential relationship dynamic. One person gets triggered, and that trigger event triggers the other person. Co-triggers happen because our nervous systems respond to each other, for better and for worse.

When both people are triggered, there can be a feeling of "Here we go again." There can be a sense of hopelessness or despair, especially if the conflict is recurring. You're going along with your day, sharing what matters to you, and bang, someone gets triggered. You may feel frustrated or angry and think, "Why are you doing that?" or "Why are you making such a big deal about that?"

When the co-trigger happens, each person has a response to the other, and their response depends on the person's typical survival responses in conflict. Do you tend to move toward, move against, or move away? These behaviors come from survival strategies and attachment patterns. How do you respond when you get triggered by something a coworker says or does? Do you move toward them, trying to understand and build connection? Do you move against them, gossiping either to them or about them, becoming hostile or combative? Or do you move away from them, trying to get space, keep distance, and avoid the conflict?

For example, a team member tells you that something you said hurt their feelings. What do you do? If you are like most people, you have a somatic response. You may notice your body tense and your breath get shallow. Now both of you are triggered, each having your own intense emotions and sensations. Neither of you is centered or grounded. Not much productive can happen here, so now what?

Another chance to practice coming back to center! In some situations, that might mean exiting the situation until you can cool off. This requires being aware of your triggers and pausing before reacting. Have you ever tried to trick yourself into thinking you're ready to talk about something, only to find out you need more time to get grounded? Giving yourself the time and space to come back to center requires rigorous self-honesty.

PRACTICE MOMENT: Investigating Your Triggers at Work

Go ahead and B.B.O.D.Y. right now. Then ask yourself the following questions:

- What triggers you at work?
- Is there a situation that always gets you?
- Who triggers you?

Once you're aware of your triggers, ask yourself:

- How will I treat myself when triggered?
- How will I be kind to myself?
- How will I speak gently to myself? (Having a few affirmations prepared is a great idea.)

Triggers at Work

Knowledge is power, but knowing your triggers doesn't mean they won't happen. Getting triggered at work sucks, but it happens to everyone, and as an embodied boss you can learn how to work with it when it happens to you.

I want to share a time when I got super triggered at work. At the time, I was teaching at a new private school that had a winter gathering for all the students and their families. This event was a cherished annual tradition. All the parents, grandparents, and various other family members were there. We all shared a delicious communal meal to celebrate the season.

This was my first year working in this community, and I had brought with me a unique tradition from my prior school where I had last taught. In this tradition, the children would walk a spiral labyrinth made of pine boughs. There were paper stars spread out along the labyrinth pathway next to the pine boughs, at regular intervals. The students would carry a candle as they slowly walked the labyrinth to the center. Then the kids would place a candle on a star. I imagined the families watching with pride as their previously feral children were calm and self-possessed. It was a beautiful ritual, and it reminded me fondly of the school I had left behind.

I entered the hall where the celebration was held. My students raced up to me, excited and dressed up. I noticed with some concern that the spiral was not yet set up, and there didn't seem to be any pine boughs present. I approached my coteacher and asked about the pine boughs, and she said she had decided we wouldn't do the spiral. It was too much effort, and she worried about how families would react.

Inside me, time stopped. At no point in the two weeks we'd been planning and practicing the evening had my colleague mentioned this. I felt disbelief and then intense rage. Without warning, I was triggered 1,000 percent.

All my students, coworkers, and families were there. My boss was there. I knew I needed to act professionally, even though all I wanted to do was yell and cry. The night continued, and I managed to fake it until I could go home and collapse.

That night as I cried, I realized I was mourning the past. I had not grieved leaving my other school and the community there. I was trying to bypass the suffering by having the new school fill that empty place.

Getting triggered at work is pretty much the worst. And yet we all get activated with some regularity. Being in a professional environment does not insulate you from the emotional experience of triggers. Maybe certain situations make you feel like an imposter. You experience microaggressions. Someone takes credit for your idea. Someone minimizes or dismisses you or what you care about. Someone talks over you. Your employee doesn't do their job, and it makes you look bad. Your idea gets shut down in a meeting. You get called out for a mistake you were hoping no one would notice. There are a thousand other ways—and sometimes, multiple things are getting poked at once!

So now what? Since you're a professional, you've got to find some way to maintain your composure until you can take care of yourself.

What to Do When You Get Triggered at Work

When you find yourself triggered at work, your primary job is to get back to center. That means focusing on what you need, and communicating that if necessary. You may be able to take care of your needs without anyone knowing you're triggered, or it may be obvious to everyone around you. Either way, it's usually helpful to get out of the situation, to give yourself time and space.

It may be difficult, but it is your responsibility to assess what the wise response in this situation would be. Then do that thing, as long as it will cause no damage. Do not send an angry email. Do not yell at the person or act with aggression. Do not think about how you're going to get revenge.

Ask yourself if you need to take a break, spend some time outside, eat a snack, or watch a cat video. Yes, I'm serious. Do what you need to do for self-care so you can calm your nervous system down and get back to center. Distraction can be helpful sometimes. Use B.B.O.D.Y. or any other grounding technique to reconnect with yourself.

Remember, when you're triggered, you are not in the present moment. Doing anything that involves your senses—like breathing exercises, or touching or smelling something—can bring you back to the now. Triggers take time to pass, and moving your large muscles can help. That's why going for a short walk is often worthwhile.

If you tend to ruminate (i.e., play the scene on repeat in your head), here is a gentle invitation to see if you can change that channel. For example, let's say you get triggered, and you determine you need to go for a walk, so you do; but during your walk, you're fuming and thinking about what you should have said. This is not helpful. Instead, place your attention on your surroundings. Notice what you see, hear, and smell. Feel your legs moving, the sun and wind on your skin. Feel your chest moving as you breathe.

Sensations and emotions will move through your system fairly quickly. Your system wants to return to equilibrium, and it will if you let it. Again, this is a lifelong practice, because this stuff is hard!

Only once you are back at center can you make your most informed decisions that you won't regret later. It's well worth it to give yourself the gift of time. You get to cultivate the skill of coming back when triggered. You don't have a choice about being triggered, but you do choose what happens next. As you continue to work with your triggers, they won't completely disappear, but they often become softer and easier to manage.

If you're a boss who cares what others think of you, you may feel ashamed that you have triggers. I want to normalize this as much as possible. You get triggered, and so does everyone else. My guess is that you also feel affected when an employee gets triggered by something you have done or said. Next we'll talk about what to do when others are activated.

What to Do When You Suspect Someone Else Is Triggered at Work

I once worked closely with a brilliant young woman named Rowen. She brought great ideas, a fantastic work ethic, and good communication skills to her work. Our work was a collaboration, but I paid her; thus, I was the "boss."

Sometimes there would be points during brainstorming meetings where she would fall silent and fold her lips inward. She never said anything, but I wondered if she was getting triggered in our meetings. I started to track my behavior. I noticed that the quiet and the lip folding would happen after she presented an idea and if I questioned it at all.

My best guess was that she felt shut down. At her quarterly review, I decided to frankly tell her that I was worried that she felt shut down by me. I asked if she would give me feedback. She agreed and said that yes, she did sometimes feel shut down by the way I questioned. For her, the questions landed as criticism. I questioned because I wanted to lean into the idea, while she received the questions as criticism.

We both had a part here. I felt grateful to receive Rowen's feedback about how my tone of voice and speediness landed for her. It was hard to hear, but the bravery she shared helped me want to get this right. It wasn't my intention to shut her down, but I could understand why she'd had that experience.

Even if I hadn't understood her point of view completely, I was willing to pay attention to her feedback and honor her experience. I started giving a slight pause after she presented something. I trained myself to write the idea down in front of her, so it would be clear I was taking it seriously. I then would gain consent from her before asking any questions: "Hey Rowen, I like this idea and have some questions. Is now a good time to ask?" Having an honest conversation about my impact helped us transform our working relationship, and it helped her have a better work experience.

If your body is telling you something is off with someone, trust it. Our nervous systems respond to each other, unconsciously picking up nonverbal cues. If you suspect that an employee is triggered at work, they probably are. Notice if you can discern a pattern to their behavior. It can be overly confronting to directly ask a person if they are triggered in the moment, so I don't suggest you start there. Instead, make space for one-on-one conversations that are low stakes. Invite your employee to have a chat because you want to check in with them about how things are going. Then ask if there is anything they need from you to do their job. On self-evaluation forms with my employees, one question I ask is: "How can I be a better boss to you?" Making folks aware that you are open to feedback creates a culture of trust and honesty.

Here are some suggestions for what to do if you think an employee is triggered at work:

- **Gently ask if something is going on.** "Hey, I noticed something seems a little off. Would you like to talk about it? No pressure, but I'm here if you need me."

- **Make no assumptions, but do make offers of support.** "I'm not sure what's going on, but I'm here to help."

- **Allow for what they're feeling.** "It makes sense that you're feeling that way."

- **Make guesses** (if that is authentic to your leadership style). "I'm going to make a guess here; did my interrupting you in the meeting upset you?"

- **Invite them to take care of their needs.** "Please do what you need to take care of yourself, and let me know if I can help."

Triggers are always going to happen, but you can become skillful in how you handle your own and your employees'. This is where the rubber meets the road as you practice somatic awareness at work.

Chapter 7 Takeaways

O You are a whole person. You (and your team) all bring your trauma to work.

O You will get triggered at work.

O Triggers happen because of overwhelming past experiences.

O You can learn to work with your triggers.

O We trigger each other.

O When you get triggered, you can practice B.B.O.D.Y.

O When an employee gets triggered (or so you suspect), you can gently ask them what's happening and offer support.

8

SOMATIC BOUNDARIES

OVER THE YEARS, I have worked with all types of couples who come to me seeking relationship support. One pair in particular stands out. Mona and Dre had founded a nonprofit together right out of grad school. They were business partners, not romantic partners. They came to me because they both felt stagnant at work and wanted to leave the nonprofit. They were willing to give somatic coaching a chance.

When they started their nonprofit, they were young and idealistic. They worked hard to create an organization in the green building industry. Fast-forward ten years, and their organization was quite successful and had done a lot of good in the field of sustainability. For the most part they got along well and had avoided the kind of conflict that can wreck a business. However, they had also avoided the conflict that would move them forward.

Mona and Dre had similar somatic bodies and strategies, which is rare in partnerships of all kinds. They were both conflict avoidant, and each of them would go to great lengths to make sure the other was happy. When I spoke with them individually, they had plenty to complain about. Unfortunately, their fear of losing the relationship prevented them from being honest with each other. Both of them had a hard time saying no.

In the year I worked with them, we first had to build a sense of safety so they could even begin to say what was true. We did many somatic practices that helped create a safer space for them to be vulnerable. The first time Dre said no to Mona, it was so hard that I thought they would leave the session.

If you cannot say no in a relationship, there are no boundaries in it. There is also no consent. If you cannot say no, you cannot say a true yes. Any yes you say must come from knowing that you could say no if you wanted to. Mona and Dre had years of not saying no under their belts. They had practiced appeasing each other for too long, and it took many practice sessions for them to build the capacity for direct conflict.

To change their entrenched relationship dynamic, their bodies had to get better at relating to each other. I'm happy to say they were eventually successful. They both still work at their nonprofit, and they now have weekly check-in meetings and have built a culture of honest communication.

All of your relationships matter. Your work relationships, especially where power is unbalanced, are particularly sensitive. You already know that humans' nervous systems affect each other. Your body is wired to respond, and it does, with or without your approval.

Part of your job as the boss is to be the bigger nervous system in the room. That means your capacity to be grounded and centered sets the tone for your team. When you become an embodied boss, your relationships improve. Solid relationships of all kinds are rooted in boundaries, consent, and listening. If you think this is overly simplified, think again. These three skills are at the root of all harmonious relationships: boundaries, consent, and listening.

As a boss, you have to say yes and no all the time. Things often move quickly—too quickly for a full-body check-in. But how do you know what to do in the moment? How do you feel enough to trust your decisions so you don't have to backtrack or change your mind later? One word: boundaries!

The Importance of Boundaries

Question: who is the worst boss you ever had?

Once you've answered that question, answer this one: what made them so bad? My guess is they had some major boundary issues. They couldn't give you clear guidance because they weren't in touch with themselves in a helpful way. They may not have respected your work or your time. They might have had boundaries for themselves but made it clear that it wasn't okay if you had yours.

The worst boss I ever had was when I was working as a ranger for the National Park Service. I was in my late twenties, when I didn't even know the word *boundary*. My boss was a woman, Michelle, who was ten years my senior. If you don't know, the NPS hierarchy models itself after the military. There is a chain of command, which means you report directly to the person above you. If you have a problem with them and try to go to their boss, that's breaking the chain of command; their boss won't talk to you, and you'll get written up. This happened to a coworker of mine whom Michelle had bullied and publicly ridiculed. Michelle was a terrible boss, yet I wasn't willing to risk my job by going over her head.

Michelle harangued anyone who did something she didn't like. She would speak negatively about them to other employees. She would throw temper tantrums. Once, when I was sick with strep throat, she called me at home to make sure I was sick and laid up. When I didn't pick up because I was sleeping, she left a message telling me I better be at work the next day since I wasn't sick.

Working for Michelle made me anxious. I never knew when she was going to erupt. The tension caused me to lie awake at night, feeling scared. Her bad bossing cost me my self-confidence. One day I realized that no job was worth feeling poorly about myself. To this day, that's the only job I've ever walked away from. When I told her I was quitting, her parting shot was, "I'll make sure you never work for the NPS again." What a relief!

Michelle had no respect for her employees, although she was able to operate just fine with her boss. This is an example of abuse of power and also of boundary failure. Being a boss people love to work for means setting and honoring your boundaries. It also means respecting the limits of your employees and the people you work with. Beyond that (the bare minimum for healthy relating), you'll need to encourage your employees to set boundaries with you.

What Are Boundaries?

Boundaries help you allow good things into your life and keep bad things out. They help you discern what's yours and what's not yours. Knowing your boundaries is how to feel your power.

When I think about boundaries, I sometimes think about a video I once saw of a new mother bear who had a bunch of cubs who were nursing. The cubs began to play with each other, still on top of the mama bear's body. The play became more and more vigorous until finally the patient mother had had enough, and she swatted one of the cubs. It wasn't severe, and it didn't cause harm, but it was firm enough to get the message across: "Knock it off." She asserted her boundary, and the cub stopped.

Think of yourself as the mama bear of your own life, both at work and elsewhere. Clear work boundaries prevent burnout. They prevent resentment from building up. They prevent you from having to leave a relationship or a situation to take care of yourself—because you will already be doing it!

Boundaries are limits. You set many boundaries in your life—with your work, your parents, your children if you have them, your colleagues, your pets, and yourself around time and money. You set boundaries in all your relationships. You can have firm boundaries in one area of your life and not another. You can hold different boundaries with different people. Boundaries are how you take care of your needs.

A boundary is typically not something you set and forget. It would be great if you could name your limit one time, and then you were golden. But people will inevitably test your boundaries. (If you've ever been around a toddler, you know this.)

The key is accepting responsibility for upholding your boundary. You cannot make your limit someone else's responsibility. For example, you tell your best friend, "I don't want to get calls after ten p.m." A week later, they call you after ten p.m. You don't answer and say, "Why are you calling me?" You simply don't answer the phone. The next day, you can remind them of your boundary.

When you were a kid, were you allowed to say no? Were you allowed to say, "I disagree. I will not. I don't want to. Stop." Were your boundaries respected? Because that's what children need to feel safe and empowered.

Children who grow up not having their boundaries respected, or who were not taught they had the right to set boundaries, often grow into adults who have difficulties setting and keeping boundaries.

To sustain relationships, you need boundaries. Boundaries offer clarity. Want to make sure your relationships within your team are strong? Practice the art of boundary setting. When you communicate what is okay and what is not okay to your team, you help them manage their expectations. You help them know how to do their job. The good news here is that boundaries are completely learnable, as you get in touch with your own feelings and needs.

PRACTICE MOMENT: Feeling for a Boundary

Think of a time when an employee pushed your boundary. How did you know? What did it feel like?

Invite that sensation to be present in your body.

What happens inside? What do you notice?

Your body will help you know your boundaries. You can feel when a limit is being pushed. You may notice anger. Anger is a great sign that a boundary needs attention. You may notice an internal sensation of pressure or pushing back.

When you feel pushed, name it: "I notice I am feeling some internal pressure about your request for next week off."

Feeling your boundaries involves paying attention to nuances you experience inside. What feels right for you? What doesn't feel okay? Pay special attention to the "uh-oh" feeling. It's a good alarm system indicating that something is off. Slow down and name what is.

Problems with Boundaries

There are four different types of problems people have with boundaries, and sometimes people have more than one. You have your boundary issues, and your employees have theirs. I'll briefly mention the four problems and then go into more depth about the strategies that create these problems. As you read through these, notice what you think your areas of growth might be.

Some people cannot say no. They can't find their voice, causing them to lose their connection with themselves. Here, the strategy is *appeasement*. They try to make others happy with them. They don't want to deal with the disappointments, frustration, or anger of others, so they don't say no.

Some people cannot hear no. They just don't or won't listen to it. This is a strategy of *nonconsent*. This is also a (yucky) sales strategy. They try to control the behavior of others by forcing their will upon them. They disregard the boundaries of others. They hate being rejected and can't stand disappointment.

Some people cannot say yes. They have a problem giving permission. Here the strategy is to *resist* everything. Sometimes people respond by saying no to every request in order to provide themselves with more time to assess. They say no first and then think it over. They can't say yes to themselves, and they can't say yes to you.

Some people cannot hear yes. They *can't receive* life's bounty. Even if they are being plied with compliments, gifts, or promotions, their strategy is to not accept. Something about receiving feels unsafe to them.

What about you? What are your challenges with boundaries? What are your strategies? Let's look at the strategies that go along with these boundary problems.

Appeasement

If you are someone who has trouble saying no, your strategy is to appease. You do what someone else wants in order to keep them happy and avoid conflict. While this may seem to have positive outcomes in the short term, all strategies have costs and benefits. Appeasing costs a lot in your relationship with yourself.

It's not a big deal when you do what someone else wants when the stakes are low. For example, you would prefer Italian for dinner, but your friend wants sushi. You agree to go for sushi. This will not significantly affect your relationship, especially if, at other times, your friend goes along with what you want. But if you never get what you want, that's a high price. Or if you repeatedly do things you don't want to do, that is a high-cost strategy.

There can be compelling reasons to say yes to something you don't want: a certain kind of safety, a feeling of belonging, avoidance of conflict. But there's a high cost when you break trust with yourself. Over the long term, it adds up. It becomes more difficult to know your desires and trust your intuition. You lose sight of what's good for you and what isn't, what's safe and what's unsafe. You violate your boundaries. This is not to blame you or pathologize you. When you developed these strategies, probably when you were young, you had good reason. You were trying to keep yourself safe.

Not trusting yourself is the result of boundary violations. Trauma-informed professional support can help you learn how to say no and feel safe.

Nonconsent and Control

Being controlling is another strategy that causes problems in relationships and in the workplace. If you're a boss who struggles with hearing no, you probably have a controlling approach. Like appeasement, being controlling is an attempt to create safety and stability. You want things to be the way you want them to be.

Like all strategies, this one has costs and benefits. It's not until the costs outweigh the benefits that you might find yourself being willing to work with it. If being controlling creates discord in your relationships, it's time to explore other options for feeling safe. One place to start this exploration is in your body. What does it feel like inside when the urge to control strikes? Many people tell me they feel tight or contracted. These body sensations are a clue you aren't feeling safe.

As children, we had very little choice about and control over our safety, so it's understandable that some of us develop these strategies. But as an adult, you get to find ways to feel safe. You get to claim your agency so you can feel sovereign over your own life and your own body. Fundamental safety is not found in controlling the behavior of others. Safety is found by first acknowledging your own needs and then being able to act on your behalf. You can create safety for yourself by noticing your body tension and then, with compassion, turning your attention to your controlling impulse. Ask yourself, "What do I need right now?" You will find that the real answer is something other than, "I need to control my employee's behavior."

Resistance

If you're a boss who struggles with saying yes, you have difficulty granting permission to yourself and others. There may be something that feels good, safe, or protective in saying no as your default response—a strategy I call an "insta-no." Some people need to say no to everything first to ensure they have the space and time to consider their options. They may have a fear of giving up control. They don't want to feel trapped in unpleasant situations, so the way to ensure that they never feel trapped is to say no to everything. Resisters need more time to make up their minds, and they feel pressured when asked to decide quickly—hence their strategy of resistance.

If this is you, you're being invited to practice discernment. You get lots of chances to practice discerning between a real no and an insta-no. Give yourself permission to change your mind. You can say yes later, or you can say yes now—and if you decide later on that you don't like your answer, you can change it. For example, if you're at an event that you aren't sure you want to be at, you can leave; and then, after leaving, if you change your mind and decide you want to come back, you can do that. If you say no to the idea proposed by someone you manage, you can consider it later and then come back and tell them you've changed your mind.

Nonreceiving

If you're a boss who struggles with hearing yes, at some point it has probably been unsafe for you to allow anything to come into your sphere. Perhaps saying yes has backfired in the past, leading to disappointment and discouragement. Even if your team is excited and saying, "Yes, let's do this," you mistrust their enthusiasm. Do they really mean no? Are they trying to trick you? Is there something you're not seeing that will cause this good thing to fall apart later? These are all fear responses.

This particular boundary issue is around trust. You also might feel concerned about a sense of obligation. If you allow yourself to receive, you could feel obligated to something or someone else. Your work is to learn to trust the yes of others. You can learn to hear yes and take a risk in trusting that it really means yes. For example, let's say you ask someone you manage to stay late to finish a project. They say yes, but then you fear they will be resentful and not do what they promised. You decide to check in later, and that check-in actually creates the resentment you were afraid of, because your employee senses you didn't trust them. In this case, you could choose to practice hearing the initial response to your request as if it were true. When the impulse strikes to check in, you could try leaning into trust: "They said yes. I am going to trust that they meant that."

Honoring Employees' Boundaries

When an employee says a clear no to you, thank them. They trust you to respect their boundaries. People set boundaries in many different ways, and many struggle to be clear. Some may feel bad for setting a limit or worry about the impact. Trust that if an employee says no, there is a good reason.

A friend once told me, "You can ask for anything if you are okay with hearing no," but sometimes people are afraid of feeling disappointed. Often we can be so afraid of hearing no that we don't even ask. Perhaps we're worried we might cross a boundary or get an undesired result, so we spend all our energy trying to predict the other person's thoughts and feelings rather than ask them directly.

Your brain also loves to make other people's boundaries about you. It says, "I am the reason they have to set the boundary in the first place. Something's wrong with me." (This is seldom true.)

Here's the deal: building the capacity to hear no and be okay is indispensable in your work toolkit. You get to work with your feelings of rejection. You get to be okay feeling disappointed when you don't get what you want. To be a boss who honors boundaries, you have to be a boss who is okay hearing no.

Honoring others' boundaries is a learnable skill. It may surprise you to learn that hearing no can sometimes feel good! It feels good because the person saying no is being honest with you. You know they're not secretly enduring something. You know they have healthy self-esteem. They aren't giving you what you want out of obligation. Getting a clear no is a gift. It's a sign of healthy communication and trust.

Setting Boundaries

There are an infinite number of ways to set a boundary. Boundaries can be both verbal and nonverbal. Verbal boundaries are the ones you say out loud. It can be as simple as "no," "stop," "don't," "I won't," and "I'm not comfortable with that." Any time you put your limits into words, you're setting a verbal boundary. Setting a limit doesn't mean you're hurting someone. This is an important nuance.

Nonverbal boundaries are expressed through your body language. Putting your hands up signals no worldwide. Crossing your arms in front of your chest says, "I am not interested or open."

Another nonverbal boundary is not responding. When someone texts you and you don't reply, that's a nonresponse boundary. I want to emphasize here that I am not recommending this type of boundary setting; I'm merely saying this is one way to set a boundary, albeit not a particularly clear one.

You want to align the verbal and nonverbal messages you send. I had a client once whose body and words did not align when she set a boundary. She would say yes but shake her head no. The reverse was also true: when she said no, she would nod. Boundaries can be scary when you first set them, and she coped with this discomfort by sending mixed messages. No wonder her team was confused.

When you set a boundary, you need no justification for it. Saying no doesn't have to make sense to anybody but you. Sometimes our boundaries are in conflict with what we think we should do or what someone wants us to do. Your body sends the "no" signal, and you're like, "What? Why is that a no? My mind is telling me I'm supposed to do this thing!" I can't emphasize this enough: listen anyway. You are building trust with your body.

PRACTICE MOMENT: Boundary-Setting Risk Assessment

If setting boundaries is sometimes scary, think about assessing the risk of setting boundaries versus not setting them. Maybe your boss has been giving you duties outside the scope of your contract, and you need to set a limit. You don't want to confront them, but you have to because you can't complete the work. Risk assessment helps you predict the costs and benefits of setting a boundary.

Now think of a situation in your life where perhaps a resentment is building, you're feeling overwhelmed, or you suspect that setting a boundary might be a good idea.

What will likely happen if you set the boundary? Make a list.

What will likely happen if you don't set the boundary? Make a list.

When you analyze the costs and benefits of setting or not setting the boundary, what do you find? Think about all aspects of the outcome, including effects on your relationship with the other person, your relationship with yourself, and your overall well-being.

How to Feel Your Boundaries

You learn what and where your boundaries are by paying attention to your body. Sensations and emotions let you know you have a boundary. Tightness, anger, edginess, irritation, contraction—these are all cues from your body that you need something.

Let's examine how your boundaries are intrinsically connected with your needs. Everyone has a similar set of needs (see the "Resources" section at the end of this book for the fantastic list of needs compiled by the Center for Nonviolent Communication). Needs are a loaded concept, and many of us have a lot of baggage about having them. But the truth about needs is that they connect you with yourself. When you start to allow yourself to feel your needs, you can also feel your boundaries.

Let me give you an example of how this works. Naila, someone you supervise, consistently shows up five minutes late to your weekly Zoom one-on-ones. They are always apologetic, and they have a good reason. Still, you notice a growing irritation inside you. When you investigate the irritation, you notice that you're feeling a tightness in your belly, and heat moving up from your belly to your chest. You notice that you clench your jaw. As you sit with these sensations, you notice that you have an internal conflict. You would like to express to Naila that their lateness bothers you, and you want to ask them to correct it. However, your workplace has been attempting to dial back a sense of urgency as a way to dismantle white supremacy at work. A part of you is concerned that if you say something, you will both participate in a system that you don't want to participate in, and you'll create conflict with a valuable employee.

So you say nothing to Naila, and resentment builds.

If you view the information that your body is sending you as valuable, you can ask yourself what needs you have that aren't met when Naila shows up late. You discover that beneath your irritation, you have a need for consideration. Your needs for mutuality and respect are also unmet.

As a wise boss, you realize that resentment is a relationship killer. With the information you've gathered from your body and from understanding your own needs with compassion, you can set a boundary that protects both you and Naila.

It could sound like this: "Naila, I notice that you've showed up five minutes late for the past four meetings. I noticed myself getting irritated, so I took a moment to ask myself what I needed. I need to feel considered and like I matter to you. Would you be willing to hear my suggestion for how we can meet in a way that doesn't increase urgency and also meets my need for mutual respect?"

Naila nods and says sure.

"Okay," you say. "I suggest that we start meetings with a five-minute window of arrival for either of us. And at the five-minute mark, if either of us isn't there, the meeting is canceled, and whoever was late is responsible to reschedule at a time that works for both of us."

We often try to talk ourselves out of how we feel. You tell yourself it's okay; you can bear this discomfort and say nothing. However, your embodied leadership presence is dependent on you listening to and investigating the information your body sends you. Slowing down to feel, and then to explore what your need is, helps you feel connected with yourself—and ultimately more connected with others.

PRACTICE MOMENT: Feeling for the Need behind Your No

Take a moment to imagine that someone asks you to do something you don't want to do, or to remember a moment from the past when this occurred.

What do you feel inside? It might be something that says "yuck" or "I don't want to."

Where do you feel that?

Can you connect with what you need? If you need to, consider the list of needs presented in the "Resources" section.

When Someone Crosses Your Boundary

Sometimes you only learn about a boundary once it has been crossed. When a boundary is crossed, your body will respond with sensations and emotions to let you know. Anger is a great sign that you have a boundary that needs your attention.

It's also important to note that we can often get triggered when our boundaries aren't respected. Many of us carry especially emotionally charged experiences from our past in which our boundaries were crossed. When certain limits get crossed in the present, this can trigger the trauma responses we talked about in chapter 6, requiring extra tenderness and care.

Boundary crossings can result in trauma. The somatic sensations you feel when a boundary is crossed may feel similar to a trigger. The difference is that boundary crossings are in the present, and triggers arise from past unresolved experiences, which may include an unaddressed boundary crossing.

Many years ago, I was taking a class in somatic awareness. One night when I came home from class, someone crossed an important boundary of mine that also had a trigger attached to it. Because I was learning about tracking sensations and emotions, I used the opportunity to observe myself in action. After it was over, I made notes.

The boundary-crossing/trigger sequence went like this:

FIVE SECONDS IN: SENSATIONS

- I feel a hot wave rising from my core through my chest and throat.
- I feel the muscles in my neck contract, my jaw clench, and a sense of tightness in my chest.
- I feel tingly at my extremities.
- I sense a "speeding up" inside my body.

TWENTY SECONDS IN: EMOTIONS

- anger
- fury
- frustration
- helplessness
- aggression

TWO TO THREE MINUTES IN: NOTICING

- My emotions are out of proportion to the situation.
- I am in a reactive mindset.
- I have a strong fight response. I want to write angry emails. I want to kick some ass.

SIX TO SEVEN MINUTES IN: CHOOSE TO B.B.O.D.Y.

- deep breathing

- grounding
- scanning my body, releasing contracted muscles

EIGHT TO TWENTY MINUTES LATER: OBSERVE BODY RESPONSES

- I feel the sensations recede, followed a bit later by the emotions starting to diminish.
- I recognize that this boundary violation triggered past trauma.
- I decide to wait to respond until my grounded self is back online.

SIXTY MINUTES SINCE BEGINNING OF TRIGGER: FIGHT RESPONSE COMPLETION

- I take a shower.
- I ask my partner to help make sure I have completed the fight response so there won't be additional trauma stored in my body. He holds a pillow while I push at it until I feel complete.

TWELVE HOURS AFTER THE TRIGGER:

- I write down these notes.
- I write in my journal about choosing to respond instead of react.

I share this as a fascinating peek into what our bodies do when boundaries are crossed and we get triggered. You can use any opportunity for practice. I recommend taking the time to do a similar observation practice the next time a boundary of yours is crossed or you are triggered. Paying attention to what your body is telling you can provide you with incredible insight about what you need to do to take care of yourself.

What to Do When Your Boundary Is Crossed

Earlier I said that boundary crossings and triggers can feel somatically similar. The processes for addressing both are also similar.

You're responsible for upholding your own boundaries, and if a boundary gets crossed—either because someone crosses it, or you fail to uphold it in the moment—it is a kindness to yourself to make sure it gets addressed.

Here are four steps you can use when something in the past triggers you, or you're dealing with a current boundary crossing.

Four Steps to Support a Boundary Crossing or Trigger

1. **Acknowledge it.** Either out loud or internally, name to yourself what's happening. Don't pretend it isn't happening.

2. **Take a break.** Don't try to do any work, have a conversation, or resolve anything. Give yourself some time.

3. **B.B.O.D.Y./return to center/ground and seek support if needed.** By allowing your body to be a place of refuge, you can calm yourself and regulate your nervous system. Sometimes you may need the support of a friend, therapist, or loved one to help you regulate. This is called co-regulation, where a dysregulated nervous system (yours) receives kindness and support to regulate from a calmer nervous system (theirs). We help each other co-regulate all the time.

4. **Deal with the situation.** Once you feel back at center, you can make good choices about how you want to respond to the boundary crossing or trigger. You have access to a much fuller range of choices from here.

Complete the Response

One thing you may choose is to complete the somatic survival response you had. Completing the response allows your body to discharge the fight-or-flight impulse and helps you avoid creating trauma that could be stored in your body.

You can complete the response by asking your body what it wants and needs. Do you need to complete a flight response? If so, either run or imagine yourself running away and outpacing the threat. Shaking and bouncing your body is a helpful way to release the flight energy.

Do you need to complete a fight response? You can push firmly against a wall or a pillow someone is holding, punch a punching bag, or smash a medicine ball at the gym.

This may sound silly to you, but I suggest that next time you get triggered, try completing a survival response, and see for yourself what happens in your body when you do it. Many people feel a sense of ease when they complete a survival response.

The truth is, some people will still cross your boundaries, no matter how good you get at setting them. But the firmer and more consistent you can be about your limits, the more likely you are to be heard. Even when your boundaries are crossed, you can feel secure that you took care of your side of the street—and you'll see where you need to set additional, stronger limits. Also, no matter what your intentions are, you will inadvertently cross someone's boundaries; and in chapter 9, you'll learn what to do when that happens.

Chapter 8 Takeaways

○ You can't be a great boss without great boundaries.

○ Having boundaries is the art of saying no clearly while remaining connected.

○ Your limits will be crossed, no matter how good you get at setting them.

○ Your body helps you know your boundaries. It's a felt-sense thing.

○ Tightness, anger, edginess, irritation, and contraction are there to help you recognize a need you are needing to take care of with a boundary.

○ You are responsible for your boundaries.

9

CONSENT—
THE SECRET TO BEING
A LEADER PEOPLE LOVE

YOU'RE READING THIS because you care about being an unforgettable boss—in a good way. You want to inspire the people you work with.
You want to help them reach their full potential as employees.

People long for ethical leadership. You get to be a leader who embodies
your power by knowing your boundaries. You get to develop the body of a
leader. This allows you to respect the limits of your team members.

If you cannot respect your own boundaries, it will be tough for you to
manage others. If you can't respect your employees' boundaries of no and
yes, they won't want to work for you. And if you really don't want to do the
boundary thing, you may want to reconsider being a boss!

One of the tricky things about boundaries is that they're very subjective. The limits you have are not the same ones your employees have.
It is not enough to simply treat people the way you wish to be treated.
That approach doesn't take into account each person's unique experiences,
needs, background, sensitivities, and privileges or lack thereof.

So how do you honor the boundaries of others? How do you know what someone's boundaries are? You ask for their consent.

Consent in the Workplace

Consent gets a lot of airtime in conversations about sexuality and relationships. You may have only thought of consent as it relates to sex. But what about leadership? So much of consent culture translates to the workplace. You can weave consent into the culture of your organization. An embodied boss is one who practices consent.

Let's talk about what consent is and what it is not. Consent happens when two or more parties, both present and sober, give their permission for an activity to occur between them. Consent presupposes that both parties can say no and that they choose to say yes. Consent is usually given verbally but can be nonverbal as well.

If I say, "May I call you tomorrow?" and you say, "Sure," we have created a consensual agreement. If I say, "May I call you tomorrow?" and you say, "I'm not available tomorrow," we have not attained consent. If you add, "But how about I call you on Friday instead?" and I agree, we have completed the negotiation. We have consent.

Defining consent gets tricky within power differentials, like the one between a boss and an employee. If you need something finished by a specific time and it's within your employee's scope of duties, and you are both fully aware of these terms, obtaining their consent is not required. You don't ask someone to consent to do their job. You can make it sound like a choice—"Hey, could you get me that document by the end of today?"—but it's not an issue of consent.

At work, consent is negotiated chiefly through the contract process. When someone is hired, you give them a clear job description and terms of compensation. The contract includes the number of hours worked per week, policies governing time off, wages, and benefits. The agreement determines the employee's responsibilities, and by accepting the job, they consent to performing these responsibilities to receive their compensation.

If the employee does not agree with something, the time to negotiate is before signing. Contracts are the written documents that emerge from a consent negotiation process. However, job descriptions rarely contain all the granular details of a job. There will be times when you ask an employee to do something that is not spelled out explicitly but is held within the spirit of the contract agreement.

There are also times when you'll have to ask an employee to do something outside the contract to which they have consented. Bosses do this all the time as new organizational needs emerge and someone has to meet that need. (We'll discuss how to make requests below.)

Because of how the power hierarchy works, it's complicated for employees to say no to bosses. They often worry they will lose the boss's respect and be accused of not being a team player. They fear that saying no will reflect poorly on them or affect future opportunities. At the most extreme end of the spectrum, they worry they will lose their jobs. This is true of people at all levels of the organization; people with a great deal of executive power also fear saying no.

When you do need to ask an employee to do something outside their contractual obligations, the best practice is to truly ask them, rather than demand that they do what you want. You can make them aware of the organization's emergent need, and explain to them why you've chosen to ask them to perform this task. Be available to work with them on their timeline, instead of enforcing your own. Remember that you don't know everything your employee is holding, both personally and professionally. You can get curious and ask what impact the request would have on their life, if they were to fulfill it. You can collaborate with them in figuring out how to get it done in a way that will work for you both.

Remember back in chapter 5 when you explored power and power dynamics? Well, consent is one practice of power-with. By including consent as a value of your work culture, you're saying, "Your feelings and thoughts matter. I care about you." You're ensuring that your employees are consenting and that they're buying into whatever task or project is on the table. When you share power in this way, your employee feels like they matter, and they feel their own sense of agency. They know they can say no, and that if they do, it will be respected. This makes a working environment collaborative.

PRACTICE MOMENT: Who Is It Hard for You to Say No To?

Take a moment to consider who you have a hard time saying no to. Your partner, if you have one? Your best friend? A parent? A pet? Your child? A coworker?

As you consider who it's hard to say no to, draw at least one breath of compassion for yourself. Boundaries are hard!

Creating a Culture of Consent

Creating a culture of workplace consent goes beyond contract negotiations. People with more power in an organization must understand the impact of asking an employee to do something beyond their duties. You empathize with the person you're asking, and you know it would be challenging for them to say no. You develop a high degree of mindfulness about making such requests.

How do you generate consent in the workplace? First, you normalize talking about power. You let your employees know your expectations. You tell them you'll check in about anything outside the scope of your agreement. Given a choice, many employees will choose to go above and beyond the defined scope of their work. They believe in the mission of the organization, and they want to be part of its success. There will also be times when an employee may want to say yes, but for some reason they cannot. That has to be okay.

You must deliberately create a workplace culture in which employees know it's safe to say no to their boss. You will need to let your team know that you expect them to care for themselves. Although you may sometimes ask for additional tasks or earlier deadlines, you acknowledge that you don't know the nitty-gritty details of their lives, and you understand that sometimes they need to say no. You will trust that when they do say no, they have a good reason for it, which you don't need to hear.

"No" is a complete sentence, and they don't need to justify their choice to you.

Saying no is hard, even when we're given explicit permission. Most employees will still justify their nos to you; no one wants to seem like that jerk who just says no and walks away. Your team will need to repeatedly hear you say, "It's okay to say no to me." Let me say that once more: your team will need to hear "It's okay to say no to me" again and again.

In practice this can sound like:

Boss Maggie: Hey Max, would you be willing to work overtime every night this week? Our deadline is Friday.

Max: Uh, yeah, I guess. [reluctantly saying yes, even though he has a family obligation and a friend hangout scheduled]

Boss Maggie: Hmm. I hear you say yes, but I'm registering some hesitation. Remember, it's okay to say no to me.

Max: Well, I have something Tuesday and Friday nights.

Boss Maggie: Okay. Are you free the other nights and willing to work late?

Max: Sure.

Creating a workplace built on consent is a radically different paradigm than what most of us have operated in. When you tell employees it's okay to say no to you, they may not believe it at first, or it may take them a while. It takes time to build trust. Those first few nos that you receive are so precious. Your employees are building confidence that you mean it when you say you care about their consent. On your end, you're practicing trusting your employees. Employees who feel your trust are more honest.

Consent builds connection and care when it's consistently practiced over time. Consistency is critical. You're all learning new skills, and this can be a vulnerable time for everyone. If someone takes you at your word and tells you no, and you still get mad, that would mean you've broken trust. In that scenario, you would need to acknowledge what happened and then repair it with the person. (We'll discuss repair in chapter 11.)

PRACTICE MOMENT: Consent at Work

For this practice, you'll explore your felt sense of both consent and dissent at work.

Find a quiet location, and take several moments to B.B.O.D.Y.

Once you feel present and inside of yourself, call to mind a moment when your consent was honored in the workplace—a time when a boss heard your no respectfully, or when you felt like you had a real choice when asked to perform a task.

Notice the feelings and sensations. What does having your consent honored feel like? Note where you feel things in your body.

Most likely, your needs for autonomy, respect, and independence, and your need to matter, are being met. Check it out; do you agree?

Let that experience go, and call to mind a time at work when your consent was not considered. Perhaps you were told to do something without being asked, or you were required to do something outside your contract that you didn't agree to.

Again, notice the feelings and sensations. What information is your felt sense sharing with you?

What needs were unmet in this situation? They're probably the same ones we just listed, as well as your needs for ease and fairness.

Let this go.

Contrast the two sets of information—your consensual experience and your nonconsensual one.

To complete this practice, invite in empathy for when your needs were unmet, and ask yourself if there's anything you need now to heal this episode of lack of consent.

Drawing Out Dissent

It would be great if all your employees set clear yes and no boundaries, but the truth is they won't because they're under your dragon tail. Or perhaps they haven't all gotten to a place inside themselves of power-within. Even in the healthiest workplace culture, you will probably never know the true extent of your impact on your employees. You have to be a bit of a mind reader, or at least an interpreter of signs, to know when someone is not saying no but wants to.

I was once communicating with an employee of mine about a time-sensitive manner that needed to be completed that day. We were chatting about it on Slack. At my company, my employees weren't required to work specific hours as long as they completed their agreed-upon work. I knew she had plans that day, and I made the assumption that a phone call would be a quicker way to communicate. I asked her for a brief call, and she quickly typed, "No, not today" but just as quickly deleted the message and retyped that she was available. She apparently was assuming I hadn't seen her first message. From that interaction, I gathered that she felt she couldn't say no to me, at least not in that moment.

Employees will cross their own boundaries. This is an impact of trauma, which we have all experienced to some degree as people conditioned in this culture of striving. Some of us are more conditioned to say yes than others due to our unique family and other circumstances. Perhaps you ask Melia to work on Saturday. She knows she'll miss her son's soccer game if she does, but she bites her lip and says okay. She's scared of what will happen if she doesn't.

A bitten lip, pressed-together lips, tightened body language, something that feels off in the tone of their voice when they say yes but want to say no—these are somatic tells. In response to them, you catch a vibe. The more embodied you are as a leader, the more in tune you'll be with these kinds of nonverbal signals.

In situations like this, you understand that they may not have given you a big wonderful yes, but you can rely on them to set their own boundaries because you've told them they can say no—right? Wrong.

Getting to consent is first about drawing out dissent. If you notice that Melia is saying a yes that sounds like a no, get curious about it. "Melia, you're saying yes, but it feels like something is up. What's going on?" This gives her a chance to move more slowly. Maybe she tells you she has an important commitment on Saturday. But if you don't yet have this level of trust and honesty, you can always make guesses. "Something feels like it's up. Can I make a guess?" If she says yes, then you can offer, "I'm guessing perhaps you have something on Saturday. Can you help me develop another way to solve this problem?" Inviting her to help you find a solution gives her agency.

Don't be afraid of dissent. Draw it out! You can only get consent when everything is on the table.

It's important to note that there is a difference between not being able to do something and not wanting to do something. As a boss, be careful about making assumptions. When in doubt, ask. An employee may want to say yes, but something may be preventing them from doing so. Because of the power differential, you can practice receiving an employee's no as if it were gold. You can be gently curious and ask if something is preventing them from saying yes, but tread carefully. If you want to create a culture of consent, you can lean into trusting the no without a justification.

When my son was a young teenager, he was required to do certain chores to be a contributing member of the family. He didn't want to do chores at all. Because he's my kid, he would say things like, "I don't consent to do the dishes," or "I have a boundary around taking out the trash."

He was able to perform those tasks, but he didn't want to. However, we weren't asking him to consent. Instead, we used our authority as parents to ensure that he participated in family life. There was no choice for him. The power differential between us would make it confusing if we made it look like a choice. Asking him, "Son, are you willing to do the dishes?" wouldn't work. We helped him understand that there were times when we took his preferences into account, and there were other times when he had to accept our authority. Doing the dishes is a nonconsensual decision. Now scrub those pots and pans!

As a boss, be clear about whether you're asking for consent or not. Sometimes you'll tell an employee what to do; sometimes you'll give them a choice. Communicate the distinction. For example, I once worked with a medical clinic that had historically been open on the weekends to serve their patients. However, COVID caused them to be understaffed, and they were scrambling to fill shifts. Two medical assistants (who have less access to power in the medical hierarchy) said they would no longer work the required one weekend per month, although it was in their contracts. They asked to renegotiate the terms of their contracts.

In this instance, management decided to enforce the contractual agreement without discussion. The two medical assistants were told they had to work weekends. In response, one of them gave notice and resigned, leaving the clinic with an even bigger problem.

When talking about consent, we're talking about power. A culture of consent is about sharing power throughout the organization. My recommendation in the clinic's situation would be to bring the problem to a team meeting and ask the staff how this issue could be solved. Presumably the staff cares about serving patients, as well as meeting their own needs. Perhaps there was another medical assistant who would have liked to work extra weekends, in order to be at home with their kids during the week. Perhaps the clinic could have adjusted the weekend schedule so it could meet its need to serve clients, while also meeting staff needs for—well, what did the two medical assistants need? We don't know, because that conversation didn't happen.

I'm not suggesting that you create jobs around people. I'm suggesting that part of consent is understanding the needs of all involved parties. Once you understand those needs, you can craft elegant solutions that meet everyone's needs.

This is almost always possible. There are times when it's not, but with more shared power and more conversation, it is indeed possible to get very creative with problem solving.

PRACTICE MOMENT: Drawing Out Dissent

For this practice, find a few minutes of undisturbed time. This is a practice that utilizes the power of your creative imagination.

Do the B.B.O.D.Y. practice.

Once you feel present in your skin, call to mind a time at work when a manager asked something extra of you, and you wanted to say no but you didn't think you could without threatening your job.

Notice any sensations happening in your body as you recall your dissent.

Remember what happened as a result of that situation.

Now, imagine you have a chance to do it again, except this time, you feel empowered to share your concerns and hesitations.

In this practice, imagine your boss as embodied and skillful. Notice that they're interested in hearing what's true for you.

Imagine telling your boss what needs you're meeting when you say no, and what needs would be unmet were you to say yes.

Notice what happens in your body as you voice your concern to your boss.

Imagine that they have the perfect response to what you share.

How do you feel?

Are there any stories that come up in your head about how this is possible, or completely impossible?

Now ask yourself: what do I need to be a boss who listens to dissent?

Do you need trust? Mutuality? Shared respect?

The final step in this practice is to imagine inviting someone you supervise to share their dissent.

The invitation might sound like, "I'd like to hear any concerns or hesitations you have about saying yes to this request."

Try saying it aloud, and notice what happens.

Practicing consent at work does not mean all decisions are now being made by consensus. You are still the leader, and the final call is still yours. There will be times when you need to follow your gut despite what your team wants.

Consent is interpersonal. It means you value the needs of your team equally with your own. Just like with any new practice, you won't get this right all the time. You will make mistakes. You might expect Melia to work in the evening when she has an event. You will miss her signs or ignore them. You will cross boundaries. But an embodied boss knows how to fall down and get back up with grace.

A Culture of Requests

Hopefully you're intrigued by the possibility of practicing consent at work. We've talked about the importance of saying no and hearing no as part of true consent. But how do you get a consenting yes?

As mentioned above, there will be times when you need to set a boundary with an employee about a project or deadline. You're not asking them to consent to do their job. In those moments, you can name what is. It can sound like, "Hey Delia, I need that report by the end of day Friday. Will there be any problem with that?" Writing reports is within Delia's contractual agreements, and she's known about the deadline for weeks.

However, sometimes you have to ask an employee to do something beyond their typical duties. Needs emerge, and someone has to meet them. Since part of your work as a leader is delegation, learning how to make skillful requests is part of your job.

Let me clarify the difference between a demand and a request. A demand is an unwillingness to hear no. It is a use of power-over. A request is just the opposite: you're willing to hear no, and you're using power-with when making a request. According to the principles of nonviolent communication (NVC; see the "Resources" section at the end of the book for more information on NVC), demands and requests carry very different energies.

Demand: Get me the Billings contract.

Request: Would you be willing to find a copy of the Billings contract? Do those feel different to you?

When making a request, you're considering your own feelings and needs as well as the feelings and needs of the person you're asking.

Requests let the receiver know why you're making the request and why it matters.

The NVC model teaches the following format for making requests: Feeling + need + request.

For example: "I'm feeling concerned about meeting the project deadline. Would you be willing to work late on the project this week?"

Feeling: concern.

Need: efficacy (meet the deadline) and integrity (do what I said).

Request: Would you be willing to work late?

Notice that my request is one strategy to meet my need. There are many other strategies that could meet the need. This is where consent and negotiation come in.

In a work culture of requests and saying and hearing no, an employee might respond with, "I can't stay late this week, but I hear you are worried about the deadline. On my end, I will make sure everything I need to do is complete by the deadline. Does that address your concern?"

In this case, your employee said no to your request, but they offered a different strategy in return: they would get it done without having to work late.

When you need to ask an employee to go above and beyond, framing it in the context of your feelings goes a long way toward sharing power.

PRACTICE MOMENT: Making a Request NVC Style

This is a quickie that will only take five minutes or so.

Grab your writing device.

Copy the following, and fill in the blanks. Consult the NVC lists of feelings and needs from the "Resources" section if you need help.

[Name of employee], I notice I am feeling _____ because I need _____. Would you be willing to [offer your strategy]?

Now say it out loud.

How do you feel in your body?

Imagine hearing no to your request. What happens in your body?

> Imagine hearing a negotiation in which the employee offers a different strategy to meet your need. What happens in your body?
>
> Now practice this today with someone. I suggest you practice the magic phrase "Would you be willing to . . ." as a way to make your request.

What to Do If You Cross a Boundary or Break Consent

At some point, you will do or say something that affects a team member negatively. They may experience this as a boundary violation. Ideally, they will clearly tell you that you crossed a boundary. (Note: I assume this is not an egregious boundary violation like sexual harassment. The following information is for minor boundary violations. If you have crossed a significant boundary, get professional support for the situation immediately.)

When people receive feedback that they've harmed someone inadvertently, most of them hurry to express their intentions. "But that wasn't my intention!" they cry. "I never meant to cross your boundary!" Well, I'm glad to hear that. Because if your intention is ever to violate someone's boundary, get out of the boss business and go straight into therapy. Leadership is a sacred responsibility. My point is that causing harm in the form of boundary violation is not about intention; it's about impact.

When you find out you crossed a boundary or hurt someone who has less institutional power than you, you have received an opportunity to embody your power and lead with greatness. At this point, most bosses default to defensiveness, but not you. As an embodied boss, you realize that this is your moment to shine. (You'll learn how to listen to and navigate workplace conflict in the next chapters, where you'll develop your skills for navigating difficult feedback.)

For now, if you find yourself in a position of having crossed a boundary, here's what to do: *nothing.*

I mean it. Do absolutely nothing. Give yourself the gift of watching your reactive, defensive self come up, or perhaps your collapsing, overly empathetic self. All of it, whatever happens—do nothing and watch with nonjudgment.

This is what so many people get wrong when they create harm. They rush in to fix it, but they're not ready. They move too quickly, driven by the reactive part of themselves that wants to make the discomfort go away immediately. Doing nothing gives you time to act with care and intention. Is it uncomfortable to do nothing? Absolutely. But this pause is necessary if you want to respond wisely.

You've got to observe how you operate. That's how you get skillful: by seeing the mistakes you *almost* make. You watch your habituated responses, and you stay soft with yourself. It might feel unbearable not to take action. We leader types are not always the best at staying with our feelings.

This is important! If an employee has been honest and vulnerable enough to share something hard with you, don't miss out on all the goodness and learning available to you. Consider this opportunity to watch and reflect as a gift.

The same is true if you find yourself on the receiving end of a call-out or getting canceled. Everything in you will scream for you to act and defend yourself, or perhaps place blame elsewhere. But powerful leaders don't react; they respond. Take your time. Get support. *Listen.* Don't make any moves before checking in with your trusted advisors. Wise leaders take their time, and when things around them speed up, they move slowly.

Doing nothing is not where it ends, of course. But this is where you start—with listening. Eventually, you'll take action to make repairs, and you'll make choices about how to move forward. This is the subject of the next chapters.

Chapter 9 Takeaways

- All people love being asked for their consent.
- If you ask an employee to do something beyond the bounds of their contract, seek their consent.
- Teach your employees that it's okay to say no to you.

○ Get to consent by first drawing out dissent. You want to hear what they really think!

○ When making a request, first share your feeling and need, to give the other person access to your inner world.

○ "Would you be willing to . . ." is a magic phrase.

○ If you cross a boundary, *do nothing* at first!

10

DEVELOPING YOUR LISTENING SUPERPOWER

ONE OF THE BEST LISTENERS I've met is also one of the most embodied people I know. My friend Barbara has an impressive capacity for presence. She is compassionate and nonjudgmental. She listens first and then takes a moment to respond. While I am speaking, she is listening. Years of somatic practice have given her honed attention. She feels and breathes as she listens. Barbara's embodied presence conveys to my nervous system that her full attention is on what I'm sharing. In response, I feel heard, acknowledged, and known when we speak.

Listening is the third leg of the embodied boss stool: boundaries, consent, and *listening*.

To be a good listener, you must be present. When you're present, you're in the same physical space and moment in time as the person who's speaking. You're open, engaged, and curious. You track what they're saying, taking it in without evaluation, judgment, or rebuttal.

Being fully listened to is one of the best feelings there is. One of the needs expressed by almost every client I've worked with is the need to feel heard. Being heard makes us feel acknowledged and validated. It makes us feel like our experience matters.

PRACTICE MOMENT: Feeling Heard

Feel into the experience of being heard by considering the following questions:

- When is a moment in your life when you've been deeply heard?
- Who made you feel that way?
- How did they do that?
- What did you notice in your body?

What Is Listening?

Listening is an active process. You take verbal and nonverbal information into your brain. Through your attention, you absorb the meaning of the ideas. Many people use the terms *listening* and *hearing* interchangeably, but they're different. Hearing is passive, simply perceiving sound coming in through your ears. Listening requires effort and interpretation. In conversation, you may hear the words someone is saying, but your attention may drift elsewhere. You are no longer listening.

When you're the boss, your job involves helping others develop their skills. Good bosses help their employees advance in their careers and their lives. To be a boss people love, you must learn to listen. We can all always become better listeners, in and out of the workplace. As with other practices we've discussed, listening involves lifelong learning.

Have you ever met someone who tells you a story and then tells you the entire story again? It may simply seem like an annoying personality trait until you understand that it's a strategy, most likely an unconscious one. They're afraid of not being understood. There is a core human need to be listened to and understood, and sometimes we go to extreme (and annoying) ends in an attempt to meet that need.

As a boss, listening is a colossally useful tool you have access to all the time, free of charge. But by itself, listening is not enough. You must track what your employee says and really take it in, and then, most importantly, you must remember to follow up and take action on it. Whatever they shared may be a small thing to you, but remember that everyone's experience is true for them. Even if you don't fully understand, trust that they are the best judges of their own experience. There is nothing you can do to make your employees feel more valued than listening and then taking action.

My employee Lan once approached me to talk about how laborious our meetings were. My first inclination was to dismiss the feedback. I thought the meetings were fine, and they accomplished my goals. I judged Lan, thinking that they were being whiny and nitpicky. I didn't get curious about their experience and didn't follow up, thinking there wasn't a problem.

A few months later, Lan quit. I realized that I had done a lousy job of listening. Their exit interview revealed that they didn't feel valued as an employee, which was at odds with my own experience. I appreciated Lan a lot. I learned then that when someone brings up something that seems like small stuff to me, it's not small stuff to them. I needed to do a better job of listening and following up. I lost a valuable employee because I only listened through my lens instead of empathizing and getting curious.

Listening Like an Embodied Boss

Good listening requires embodied presence. You must be grounded and centered, with your body open, attuned, and relaxed. Before meeting with an employee, you can prepare yourself by taking a few moments to B.B.O.D.Y. If you're creating a culture of embodiment at work, you might invite your employee to B.B.O.D.Y. with you if that feels comfortable, or you can begin a meeting by taking a few breaths together.

When listening, you make eye contact. You focus your attention on what the other person is saying. If your attention wanders, you bring it back. While they're talking, you don't spend the time planning what you're going to say when they're done.

People often talk on the surface of things, so as a listener, you must learn to listen beneath the actual words. You listen for meaning. Through the imperfect medium of language, they're trying to convey something meaningful, and sometimes this meaning can be hidden.

When you listen to someone, it's not that you won't have feelings and reactions that come up. This is perfectly normal. But when judgments and feelings come up, you can say to yourself, "I will attend to that later; I'm listening now." Granted, it's hard to back-burner your own experience in this way, but it's a helpful pause technique. You'll get more out of a conversation when you focus on active listening and not on your own reaction.

As an embodied listener, you speak less than you listen. You ask questions to understand more. Your body language demonstrates to the other person that you're actively listening. You turn toward them, uncross your arms, and nod your head from time to time.

PRACTICE MOMENT: Feeling Your Back Body While Listening

One helpful somatic practice when listening is to feel your back body.

Feel for your back body now. If you're sitting, press backward against your chair; if you're standing, find a wall and press backward against it. Notice the full length of your back body.

Imagine listening from back here. You can practice feeling your dimension of depth. Listening from your back body gives you far more access to embodied resources. You have more space. Try to feel it now.

The next time you're meeting with an employee, or perhaps when you're practicing with a partner or trusted friend, sit upright and press back against your chair. Find your spine. Imagine listening from the back of your brain. There's more space to hear and understand if you're not pushing forward. Try it and see.

Allowability of Feeling

An essential listening concept is simply allowing someone to feel what they feel. In practice, this is a lot harder than it sounds. Notice what happens the next time an employee brings you a difficult feeling they're having about you. How do you handle it when someone tells you they feel frustrated with your behavior? Do you immediately think their feelings are wrong? Do you get defensive, shut down, turn the blame on them, or try to change what they're feeling? All of these behaviors, even if they're just in your head, are attempts to take control of the situation rather than just letting yourself be present for another person's feelings. Hearing someone's feelings can be hard work. It's usually easier to hear people express their feelings when they're not about us.

In working with hundreds of couples, I've observed how hard it is for most people to just let others feel what they feel. We often wish the other person felt differently. We wish they didn't feel at all. We feel annoyed that they're having feelings and communicating them. We wish they felt the way we do. We especially don't like it when they feel frustrated, angry, disappointed, or betrayed by us. We immediately jump to justify our behavior or defend our intentions.

What I'm about to say may sound counterintuitive: just like the contractions we discussed in chapter 3, the quickest way for someone to move through their feelings is to acknowledge them. This goes both for others and for yourself. Next time someone you work with comes to you to let you know how upset they are with you for XYZ, try this: look at them, take a breath, and say, "I hear that you are upset with me for XYZ." That's it. Then notice what happens, both in them and in you.

Likely they will say something like, "Yeah, that's right. When you did XYZ, I felt really mad." They may share more information with you.

Reflecting back their feelings does not mean you're agreeing with their position. It doesn't mean you're saying, "Yes, I did XYZ." You heard them express their feeling, and you reflected it back to them.

You have just allowed your employee to feel the way they are feeling. You've let them know that their feelings are okay, and safe, with you.

Allowability of feeling is a pattern interruption for most of us. Few of us grew up getting these kinds of responses to our feelings, and we weren't trained to give them. It's a game-changer when we're met with validation and acknowledgment instead of pushback when we share our feelings.

Most of us feel disarmed when we're met with allowability of feeling. It's a great technique to de-escalate heated situations. It also creates an atmosphere of safety and care.

Once you get comfortable with allowing feelings at work, you can take the practice to the next level with this magic phrase: "Tell me more." It's magic because you're inviting more communication and connection. You're giving yourself the gift of access to more information, and you're giving the speaker the chance to fully express what's going on for them.

When you curate openheartedness as a listener, you can receive the other person in all their complexity. This means trying not to take what they're sharing personally (more on this in a bit). You're not thinking about how you will respond.

It can be hard to listen if you feel your need to be heard won't be met. One thing you can try is some internal self-talk: "I am going to listen to this person first, and then once they feel heard, I will ask them to hear what's important to me." It's reassuring to remind yourself that listening does not cost you the opportunity to be heard.

After they feel complete, when it's finally time for you to respond, you have taken in what they said so you can summarize and reflect back what you heard in the exact words they used. Don't expect your brain to get it all; you'll give the other person an opportunity to remind you of anything you might have forgotten. For instance, after someone shares something important to them, you can reply with something like, "Okay, cool. This is what I hear you saying: [insert what you heard them say]. Am I getting it? What am I missing?"

It's fantastic to ask that question. When you ask "What did I miss?" you allow the person to feel precisely what they're feeling without challenge. You get the chance to understand more and let your empathy come online. To be a leader people love, you need to know when to talk and when to listen.

When to Listen

Good discernment about when to talk and when to listen is based on self-awareness. If you find yourself uncertain about which strategy is required in any particular moment, you can ask yourself the following set of questions:

How much have I already spoken during this conversation? Think in percentages. Have you spoken 10 percent of the time? 60 percent? If you're actively listening, you should be talking no more than 20 percent of the time. You listen, reflect what you hear, and ask clarifying questions. That's it. This is not a time to problem-solve, share your experience or feelings, or fix anything. When you're actively listening, the only agenda you have is presence. While this type of presence is rare, it is also a tremendous gift you give to your employees.

Do I need to be the one to say this, or say this right now? No commentary is necessary when you're actively listening. You don't need to add anything or extrapolate. There might be something you need to say, but now may not be the right moment. Make a mental note to say it later.

Is there anything I don't understand that I can ask about? You can use clarifying questions to draw out dissent. You want to hear what your employee is struggling with. You want to know why they're unhappy in their role. Drawing out dissent may seem illogical—give people a space to complain, and they will, right? But when you create space for the hard stuff, you build a culture that normalizes talking about everything. This includes unpleasant or difficult topics. You're creating transparent communication and building trust. You're interrupting resentment. Resentment is a toxic relationship killer, in and out of the workplace, consisting of all the unsaid yuck. So get curious and ask those questions, draw out dissent, and listen without judgment. This is a great place for "Tell me more."

These questions should help you know when to listen and when to speak. When you're actively listening to someone, there will be a time when it's appropriate for you to talk—and discerning when is an art. If you get nothing else from this book, take this: listen first.

Mansplaining

One of the critical factors in employee dissatisfaction is feeling micromanaged. Part of feeling micromanaged is having things explained to you that you have in-depth knowledge of. You may have heard the term *mansplaining*, which is when someone with more power or privilege determines that they need to explain something without considering what the listener already knows. Everyone likes to feel valued for their knowledge, but many people experience this form of communication as condescending.

Mansplaining can be committed by, and can happen to, people of all genders, and it tends to follow lines of privilege. The word has its roots in the all-too-common phenomenon of a man telling a woman how to do something that she already knows how to do, or explaining something that she already knows about. Mansplaining also happens between men when they posture, try to access social capital, or assert dominance by professing their knowledge. If you tend to lead with talking and like to act like the expert about things, you may want to take an honest look at whether you might be a mansplainer, a whitesplainer, or any type of 'splainer. It's not a cute look on anyone.

A guy friend of mine once told me that he doesn't know when to talk at work anymore. As a high-level manager and someone who loves to debate ideas, he thought he was just talking. But he had received feedback that he was frequently mansplaining. He wanted to know how to tell the difference.

As an example, let's meet a chronic mansplainer. Mel is an intelligent guy who knows a lot about a lot. He meets a new friend, Sarah. Mel knows Sarah is interested in stained glass. Mel starts to tell her what he knows about stained glass. Likely, Mel is trying to connect with Sarah about an interest of hers. Mel tells her how to cut the glass, what pressure to use, and the best solder to buy. Mel doesn't know that Sarah has a master's degree in art history with a background in medieval stained glass, and she's an instructor at a local crafts school. Mel has missed an essential point of connection. He forgot to ask. You can imagine Sarah's eyes rolling as she listens to Mel go on.

Have you ever had an appointment with a doctor who, before they even ask what you're doing to take care of yourself, launches into a sermon on the value of exercise? If they had slowed down to ask you, you would have told them you run five days a week, and lift weights three. It feels like quite a disconnect when someone assumes they know more than you do—especially about your own situation. You can save yourself embarrassment (and potential resentment from the other person) in similar situations. Know that there is always the chance that the person you're talking to knows more about the topic than you do, but perhaps they're too polite to tell you, so they nod and wait until you're done. Track the percentage of time you're talking. If it's a conversation between two people, make sure you take up no more than half the time with your words. Less, if you're the boss!

Pro tip: your consent practice can save you from deadly 'splainer syndrome. Don't jump in and tell what you know at first. Instead, start by asking questions to find out what someone else already knows. After listening to what that person already knows, you can then speak. If you would like to share what you know, obtain consent. It sounds like this: "Are you open to hearing some information I have about the topic? No pressure." Through listening first, you create pathways for connection.

The Importance of Belonging

The best boss I ever had was himself a teacher of somatics and embodiment. The following story describes how his embodiment as a leader helped me through a hard time at work.

I worked for Joseph for eight years. As someone living with ADHD, he learned that thriving at work meant having a support person sitting next to him as he wrote curriculum, responded to emails, and developed content for his websites. He hired me for my experience with somatics as well as my capacity to organize and write coherently.

Every day when I arrived at work, he stood to welcome me. He took a few moments to inquire about my life before we sat down together to discuss what we would do that day. At many moments during our work time, he would suggest standing and stretching, or just taking a breath together. He encouraged me to take breaks as needed for food, water, bathroom, or movement. I was to attend to my body needs as part of our work together.

Joseph was always learning more from other somaticists. As a result, he would suggest we explore new practices. We would then compare notes on what we learned from these practices. Part of our work included being in our bodies together and learning to feel ourselves with greater nuance.

When I would make a suggestion that either surprised him or that he felt activated by, he would name his internal experience: "I noticed that when you said that, my heart started to pound." Sometimes he would ask what I was noticing in my body in response to the work we were doing. When I was ill, he encouraged me to stay home and take care of myself.

I write all of this to give you the context of what an embodied work-place looks like in practice. For me, working with Joseph honored my mental work as well as my body. My needs for being heard and acknowl-edged were met, as Joseph listened deeply to my thoughts and frequently took my suggestions. When we had conflict, he would often return the next day and tell me how he had explored our disagreement, and he would ask about my experience.

One thing that was a challenge in our work together was our different writing styles. My style is to get all the ideas on the screen, and then go back and edit and form coherent statements. Joseph prefers to edit as he goes. My process is much quicker than his, and I would often feel irritated with his slow speed, or with him editing as he watched me write.

We often shared documents, with both of us having editing privileges, and he might erase a sentence before I finished writing it. We both found these moments frustrating, and they occurred with some frequency because a lot of what we did was write together.

We learned that when either of us was noticing tightness in our bodies or frustrations in our emotions, it was best to name it to each other. Then we employed a strategy whereby he would leave our shared work environ-ment, allowing me to bang out a version of what he wanted. When I was done, I would call him back, and he would have the opportunity to edit. This increased the efficiency of our process and eliminated a lot of struggle between us. His embodiment let him notice when things weren't working. His embodied trust in me allowed him to step away when necessary.

When you think about the best boss you ever had, what made them great? My guess is that it wasn't just that they were the opposite of your worst boss. Under their management, you probably felt like they respected and cared about you as an individual. Your employees are not cogs in a wheel; they're not putting in time merely to further the organization's mission. They're yearning for the same thing all humans need: belonging.

Being listened to helps employees feel that they matter and they belong. Part of your managerial duty is to create a culture of belonging. This might sound a little woo-woo or feelings-y, but creating a culture of belonging is in everyone's best interest. Employees who experience a strong sense of belonging at work are satisfied enough to stick around and put in their full effort.

Do you have an open-door policy? Do you remind your team that they're welcome to come and visit your office when they need to (or if you work remotely, that they can call you when needed)? How do you feel about developing an open-door policy? If you're worried about interruptions, you can designate certain times as "deep work/no interruptions."

Your employees will be ready and willing to talk when it feels right to them—on their timetable, not yours. If you want them to bring you things, you need to be available when they're ready to talk.

I've raised two children to young adulthood. In my kids' early adolescence, another parent clued me in to the "chatty hour." Before I tell you what that is, let me say that I'm early to bed and early to rise. Nine p.m. finds me horizontal and heading toward dreams.

The chatty hour often occurs between 9:30 and 11:30 p.m. for teenagers. It's the time in their day when they're more available to connect and to share what's going on in their world. There have been countless nights where I've sat up late with my kids because one of them was in the mood to talk. To be totally honest, most of what they share doesn't seem that important to me, but profound truths emerge if I listen long enough. It helps that I'm unlikely to speak very much (because I'm tired!), but I'm available to listen. Miraculously, we made it through their teenage years with our hearts and relationships intact. I credit much of my success as a parent to learning early on when and how to listen.

Be available when your employees are, even if it's not always the most convenient for you. Be willing to listen as they wade through their thoughts. Some people are external processors and can only get to their point by talking around it for a while. There is gold there for the patient boss who is willing to wait for it.

Consider all ideas they bring to you, even if they don't seem that great at first. Even if you already know you won't implement it, listen, make notes, and give the idea a fair shake. See if you can understand why your employee thinks the vision they brought to you is good. You can consider all ideas, not be dismissive, and still make clear decisions.

If you decide not to take their idea, communicate why not. Make it clear that you value them sharing ideas with you and appreciate this kind of ownership and care.

Receiving Feedback

Receiving challenging feedback is a tricky part of your job. No one understands the pressures you're under. Those above you (your boss, if you have one; your investors; your board) want results now. Those managed by you want compassion, care, respect, dignity, and belonging—and they can be very vocal about it.

If you're an entrepreneur, it's your job to make sure all the things happen and everyone gets paid, no matter what. If you're a boss in a non-profit or for-profit, you have many duties beyond those your employees know about. Remaining empathetic to your employees' feelings can be extremely difficult when you aren't sure how you'll make payroll that week or fulfill other obligations you have. I say this to extend empathy to you for how hard it can be to receive negative feedback, especially in the midst of all the other balls you have up in the air.

As you're well aware, people will have feelings and judgments about you and your leadership. Part of their feedback will be helpful to you. But sometimes part of what they give feedback about will be their projections.

Projection is when a person displaces their feelings, thoughts, and experiences onto another. An example of projection is when an employee is frequently late with their deadlines, and then jumps all over you if you miss responding to an email as quickly as they would like. They are projecting their own feelings onto you. Therapists expect projection as a normal part of the therapeutic process, and they're trained in how to work with it; but I'm guessing you're not a therapist. Receiving projection as a boss sucks.

While a high percentage of feedback from an employee could consist of projection, there is usually a nugget of truth within the input. It's your job to dig out that nugget. Their reaction to something you did might be oversized due to their own trigger, but there was still something you did that affected them and catalyzed their response. This does not make you responsible for their reaction or feelings.

Sometimes our initial reaction to feedback is one of disbelief because we don't see what our employee sees. But it's highly possible that they observed something real that we have not yet recognized or admitted about ourselves. Acknowledge that all bosses, indeed all humans, have blind spots.

Somatically, you'll feel an impact when you receive feedback. Challenging feedback is painful, and it shows up in your body, your mood, your concentration, and your other relationships. It can be challenging to come back to the center when you feel an impact. You have emotions and sensations designed to get you out of the pain you're feeling.

Feedback is a gift, albeit one that is often hard to unwrap and enjoy. Employees who give you feedback share their feelings and needs, which can be a bridge to greater understanding and even skill after you get over the hurt.

Let's examine a situation in which a manager I worked with received negative feedback and processed it through her body. Kadyn managed a physical therapy clinic. She was in charge of nine physical therapists and the admin team. She had been working there for five years when one of the PTs asked for a meeting with her. In the private meeting, the PT unfurled a long list of complaints about Kadyn's management style, including saying they were embarrassed by how Kadyn represented the clinic professionally when speaking to potential clients.

Since this was the first time Kadyn had heard any feedback from this particular PT, she felt a significant impact from the demeaning tone she perceived during the meeting. However, she made notes of the conversation and told the PT she would need some time to reflect on the feedback and would respond the following Friday.

During that time of reflection, Kadyn and I had a somatic coaching session. Kadyn wanted to allow her body to feel the actual impact and to notice what part of it was not about here and now. During our session, she realized she had not taken a single deep breath since receiving the feedback. She felt that her diaphragm was strongly contracted as she tried not to feel the impact of the feedback. As she put her attention on her diaphragm and, with my encouragement, allowed the contraction to happen, she had a memory of being in second grade and going to see her grandmother, who said to her, "Did your mother dress you like that?" Kadyn's reaction was to feel completely humiliated. She recalled the hot wash of shame flooding her body and her determination not to be embarrassing ever again.

While much of the PT's feedback had felt reasonable, and she could understand why the PT was bringing it to her, the comment about the PT's embarrassment had hit Kadyn in a part that carried a lot of old shame about how she presented herself.

Once she acknowledged the pain from her childhood and let the grief and shame dissolve, she parsed out that part of the feedback was inappropriate and had more to do with the PT than it did with Kadyn. Kadyn felt proud about how she presented the clinic to potential clients and felt that she was in integrity with the clinic's mission.

I include this story because Kadyn couldn't move forward until she could separate what was legitimate and valid about the feedback from what was unskillful and cruel. Upon first hearing the feedback, she had a freeze response. Later, once she had clarity, she could meet the PT with skill. She responded to the feedback that would be helpful for the clinic and let the PT know that their embarrassment was theirs and that she would not be changing how she interacted with the public. The PT, hearing a clear boundary, could also move on. Ultimately, their relationship deepened based on honest and boundaried exchanges.

Your Brain on Negative Feedback

Your lizard brain is not great at discerning between real and actual threats, and it's wired to perceive negative feedback as a threat. For this reason, many folks freak out when receiving negative feedback.

A predictable series of responses follows, initiating in your lizard brain. Most of them are automatic, and none of them are beneficial. In the simplest terms, someone tells you some part of your bossing sucks, and you get triggered. You may then:

- Double down and insist that your truth is *the* truth, and the other person is wrong.
- Be dismissive (e.g., "I was just joking").
- Minimize what they're saying, or ask why they're making such a big deal out of it.
- Get defensive or try to find fault with the other person.
- Display fragility by becoming the victim of the mean feedback-giver.
- Center yourself instead of listening to whatever truth that person is sharing.

When you get impacted, your body and brain move at different speeds. Something has occurred that has caused a somatic trigger response in your body. When your brain processes something like negative feedback as a threat, you might experience:

- neurochemicals dumping into your bloodstream
- muscular contractions
- survival responses
- emotions
- changes in breathing rate and depth
- increased heart rate
- jaw clenching
- tears forming
- leg muscles getting ready to move

- chest, throat, or eyes armoring or tightening
- stomach feeling nauseous
- a change in the experience of time
- any or all of these physical sensations, plus many more

Your brain tries to comprehend what's happening by assigning a story and meaning to it. For better or worse, you have well-worn neural pathways that explain the situation. These are the narratives that pop up whenever your core wounds get poked. You receive impact, and your body responds; then your brain comes up with a story. Where does your brain usually go when you receive negative feedback? Here are some common places:

- "They did that on purpose." (betrayal)
- "Eff you! You do XYZ too!" (retaliation, lashing out, fight response)
- "That's not true!" (protection)
- "In not even the smallest way could that ever possibly be true about me!" (denial)
- "I did it wrong!" or "I'm not good enough!" (internalizing, shame)
- "They don't like me!" (rejection)
- "I need to fire them." (turning away)
- "Now they're going to leave!" (abandonment)
- "How did I miss that? I'm so dumb!" (self-abandonment)
- "I need to get out of here *now!*" (flight response)
- Brain fog, confusion, numbness (freeze response)

It's okay to be affected by feedback. Some bosses let it roll off. Some bosses take it in deep. If you take it in deep, welcome to the club!

PRACTICE MOMENT: Surviving an "Ouch"

Consider a time recently when negative feedback affected you.

- Remember the context of the moment and how you felt in your body.

- Remember the sequence of emotions and sensations that flooded through you.

- What did you do with that impact?

- How did you survive that ouch?

What to Do When Receiving Negative Feedback

First, acknowledge that you are likely triggered. Nothing good will come out of saying or doing something now that you will need to recant later. So. Just. Stop. Do nothing except B.B.O.D.Y. Breathe. Observe. Get three-dimensional. Yawn, stretch, and wiggle. Slow your roll, and take the information in. Give yourself the gift of pause, trusting that you will have plenty of time to figure out how to respond wisely.

Make an agreement with yourself to do nothing with the feedback until you are back at center. Depending on the situation, this could take a few minutes, a few hours, or a few days. Give yourself permission to take all the time you need. In the meantime, talk to supportive allies and mentors in your life. If you need them to listen to you, ask for that. If you want their thoughts about how to move forward, ask for that. Be specific about the kind of listening and feedback you want.

Have compassion for the fact that any of your instant reactions are strategies to protect you from threat and exclusion. There is no need to feel shame for utilizing these strategies. We all have them, and we all use them. What's important here is that your first reaction is not your final action. Even if you find yourself engaging in one of these protective strategies at first, you get to choose what happens next.

For instance, you can say something like, "I'm sorry, I notice I'm feeling a bit defensive. Give me a minute to take a breath. It's important to me to really hear what you're saying." Name what's happening, take a short break, and return to the listening. Any time you notice yourself engaging in a less optimal, less skillful strategy, you can name it and then come back to openhearted listening.

I'm sure you've heard "don't take it personally" when it comes to receiving negative feedback. But I'm guessing you've already tried that countless times and aren't able to. That's because it doesn't work. Trying not to take it personally is telling yourself not to feel what you're feeling. But you can't think yourself out of your feelings. When you receive an ouch, the first thing to do is to allow it. In this case, that might mean taking it personally.

Remember "allowability of feeling"? Well, that goes for you too. Allowing yourself to feel what you feel is a surprisingly effective way to be with the impact of hard feedback. When you tell yourself, "I feel this way right now," you're also trusting that this will not always be true. Feelings will shift and change. Your first reaction is not your final answer.

Feelings aren't facts. They are an experience in your body, one you can learn to make space for. They point to things that need your attention.

Five Steps to Soothe the Ouch! of Feedback

1. **Acknowledge the impact.** "Ouch! That just happened."

2. **B.B.O.D.Y.** Feel what you feel; pay attention to your emotions and sensations without judgment.

3. **Allow.** Offer yourself support and care for the impact, regardless of the ouch. You'll figure out what to do later. Give yourself ample time to come back to center before you respond.

4. **Get curious.** Once you feel more centered, bring your critical thinking skills online. Utilize support.

5. **Seek out the golden nugget of truth buried under the mountain of projection.**

Of course, you may have thick skin, and all the hard feedback might roll right off you. Please send me some of what you've got! But for all the tender hearts out there, you have my compassion. Feedback can be challenging even when it's super helpful, and by becoming an embodied boss you're developing the chops to receive it.

It's essential to create a feedback culture as part of a growth mindset, so do it—even though it hurts. Eventually, just like with weight training, you'll build some muscle. Until then, you'll get plenty of opportunities to practice your conflict skills!

Chapter 10 Takeaways

- Listening is an active, embodied practice.
- Belonging is a core need of humans.
- Listening creates belonging.
- Allow people (including yourself!) to feel whatever they feel.
- Be ready to listen when people are prepared to talk.
- Receiving negative feedback is ouchy. Take care of yourself.
- When you're ready, you can explore what's useful in the feedback.

11

NAVIGATING CONFLICT

LOU AND JEN have been best friends since medical school. Their friendship grew solid through late-night study sessions and teary melt-downs. After they completed residency, by chance they were both hired at the same clinic. Initially, they were both direct-care physicians. How-ever, after a year, Lou became the clinic manager, making her Jen's boss.

This was when their workplace conflict started. As you can imagine, there was some tension over Lou's promotion. They continued to be friends outside of work, choosing to protect their friendship by not discussing the changing power dynamic at work. Not only was Lou learning to lead, but she had a rebellious, envious staff member who was also her best friend. When Lou had her first child, she asked Jen to take time off from work, fly to Greece, and support her birth process. Jen did. They were friends, after all.

Later, when Jen developed some health issues that required her to take time off from her job, Lou became frustrated. Jen's repeated absences were having a negative impact on the team. Lou had to talk to Jen as a boss, but she couldn't; she felt too indebted to Jen. Jen, on her end, felt unsupported by Lou. She couldn't understand why Lou wasn't encouraging her to get the health care she needed. Tensions continued to build.

Lou pulled back from their friendship, again without communicating. Now Jen was extra hurt, because although she had supported Lou during her birth process, Lou wasn't reciprocating. Jen started to grumble at work. She talked to her coworkers about Lou's lack of support. Her coworkers felt caught in the middle.

Lou also stopped communicating directly with Jen. She would send factual emails without warmth. Any time she saw Jen, she would head in the other direction. The other clinic staff felt awkward and uncomfortable as Lou and Jen's conflict continued, unaddressed. When a doctor on the team finally called in HR, they couldn't successfully mediate the conflict, mainly because Lou avoided honest, open discussion, and Jen used power-under to undermine Lou's authority.

This went on for months before Jen finally left her position. As their working relationship ended, their friendship also ended. The clinic was short a doctor, right when the COVID-19 pandemic was creating tremendous need.

The lack of skills for conflict, communication, and boundaries in the workplace has enormous consequences, and not just for those involved directly. Individual team members, and team morale, take a big hit when workplace conflict goes unresolved. If Lou had had the skills to navigate conflict more effectively, the clinic could have retained Jen, and their relationship might still be intact.

What Happens during Conflict

Conflict requires three things:

- at least two people
- a disagreement or dispute over an issue for which it's possible to take opposing sides
- negative emotions

Conflict is a competition about who is right and who is wrong. People in conflict consider themselves adversaries. Lack of cooperation and antagonism are present, and other negative behaviors often emerge.

Most people get triggered during conflict, meaning there is a high chance of reactivity. Your amygdala (the fear center of your brain) fires, and you often repeat patterns you learned in your family of origin. Your conflict style is influenced by how those around you fought. That doesn't necessarily mean you do it like they did. As a survival strategy, you may have learned to do it exactly the opposite. Things that are "normal" to you during conflict may differ from what is normal to your sparring partner.

When my partner was growing up, it was acceptable to slam doors when you fought. In my family, it wasn't. We got chilly and silent instead. Today, when he and I get into conflict and he slams doors, it scares me. I go quiet, and it freaks him out. Is anything bad happening? No, not really. But our bodies are responding as if it is.

Humans have lots of conflict tactics, such as blame, hostile accusations, attacks on people's personhood, gaslighting, name-calling, and bringing up the past.

Almost everyone goes into black-and-white thinking when in conflict. We think, "I'm right, you're wrong." Again, this is how our brains are wired to behave in situations where we feel threatened. In these moments, we are not the most enlightened versions of ourselves.

The Benefits of Generative Conflict

It might seem strange, but workplace conflict can have benefits. The concept of generative conflict is a paradigm shift for many people. The basic idea is that conflict can be helpful by pointing to what's not working. It can be destructive at times, but it can also shift our unhelpful patterns. Emotions, longings, and resentments underscore most conflict, and it's easy to get stuck in these places when we're not challenged to move out of them.

The significant benefit of conflict is that hard truths get named. The things you don't say when you're not in dispute—well, now you can communicate them. You might be able to finally name those simmering resentments or get that stuck thing out in the open. You can clear things during the conflict by saying something that needs to be said.

Conflict can be beneficial to relationships. It can change how you listen to your opponent. You can train yourself to get curious and ask questions that get beneath those surface-level assumptions. You can focus on the future rather than the past. You can be wonderfully creative in how you repair.

Conflict opens our eyes, ears, and minds—and our hearts, if we're lucky. It makes us pay attention. It forces our attention toward what's happening within us, around us, and between us. There's no hiding when conflict is present.

Conflicts are teachers. They invite us to become aware of what needs healing and what we have not yet learned to handle skillfully. Conflict allows us to see what needs attention. Granted, it's not the most pleasant of experiences when it's happening. But conflict gives you a chance to get clear on your boundaries. In conflict, you get to hold on to what's most important to you.

We all get conflict training from our families of origin. When we get older, we often realize we need a different kind of training. As an adult, you get to decide who you want to be while in conflict. You get to set the boundaries for your behavior. You get to have integrity in the heat of the moment.

Here's my list of who I want to be during conflict:

- I want to retain my connection and stop and feel what's happening in my body.

- I want to respect the other person's humanity.

- I want to move slowly enough that I don't say anything mean-spirited or manipulative.

- I want to express my most honest truth.

- I want to be as responsible as possible in the moment. I know that this is not always possible, so I will always honestly seek and name my contributions once I am back at center.

- I will not hide from my suboptimal motivations.

- I want to be good at conflict.

PRACTICE MOMENT: Who Do You Want to Be during a Conflict?

Now you do it. Grab something to write with. Brainstorm a list of six to ten sentences about who you want to be during conflict.

Skill-Building for Conflict

Professional fighters, like boxers, wrestlers, and martial artists, must adhere to a code of conduct during the conflict, or else they face disqualification. They don't get to do whatever they want just because they're fighting. There are rules of engagement. They learn to direct their fight response in a responsible, respectful way. Like them, you can learn to be a great fighter.

Consider the following the embodied boss's rules of engagement:

Maintain body awareness. Surprise surprise, right? Feeling yourself is helpful during and after conflict. Your mind and your body can cooperate to handle the situation, but this is a skill you must rigorously train. You can learn how to make good choices while adrenalized, like EMTs do. Become intentional about practicing fighting with an adrenalized nervous system while retaining your integrity.

Slow down. Give yourself permission to slow down. Inside your head, it sounds like this: "Self, let's give you some breathing room and slow this down." You can B.B.O.D.Y. to de-escalate the conflict. That way, you stay connected with yourself. You feel sovereign rather than entering into a reactive attack-defend mode.

Take a break. Conflict can be triggering to most people. When you're triggered, your nervous system is dysregulated. You can give yourself permission to take a break so you can slow down. Breaks during conflict help your nervous system to become regulated. Then you can connect with your own feelings and needs, and get curious about the feelings and needs of your opponent. You don't make decisions from a triggered place.

Get curious. Invite yourself to challenge the assumptions and stories you have about who this person is and what they want. Instead of misbeliefs and judgments, invite in your inquisitive nature. What are they saying? Yes, it seems as if they're screaming about the board meeting, but what is underneath? Ask yourself, "What is going on here?"

Say "Tell me more." This simple phrase is pure gold. If you receive an ouch during the conflict and have the impulse to defend, try saying, "Tell me more about that." Instead of exacerbating the conflict by protecting, you sidestep. This is a powerful system interruption. When you stay curious and listen, you may be surprised by what comes next.

Be a boss willing to listen before you speak. We are often fighting to be understood. It's important to all of us to be known, to be seen. But it's important to recognize that there is no competition for who gets to be understood. There is enough understanding to go around. Beloved leaders try to understand first, then seek to be understood. They listen first.

Name what is. Remember back in chapter 2 when you practiced noticing sensations and emotions in your body? Naming what is is a game-changing conflict strategy. When you name what you're noticing, whether in your own body, the situation, the power dynamics, or the room, you give everyone the gift of slowing down and noticing what's happening. It can be a powerful tool to help everyone come to a shared reality. When folks are triggered and in their trauma response, the situation can be experienced as quite different from what is actually happening.

Get understood, but later. Here's the promise you make to yourself when you decide to listen first: "I will be understood. It might not be right now, but I promise that I will bring it up in another moment. I will make sure that I get understood."

Bonus: increase your capacity for discomfort. Conflict is a premium training opportunity for developing your capacity to stay with discomfort. Being with discomfort means recognizing your uncomfortable feelings and softening toward them, instead of bracing, resisting, or trying to get away from them.

PRACTICE MOMENT: Your Code of Conduct When in Conflict

You get to determine who you want to be as a fighter and what your code of conduct is. List your boundaries with yourself. These can be things like, "I will not use a demeaning tone of voice" or "I will not bring up conflict from the past."

Whatever your code for yourself is, write a quick draft now. You can refine it later.

Retaliation Is Not Your Friend

Retaliation is about power. It is an attempt to regain control when you feel like a victim. You externalize your pain and try to hurt someone else. Revenge is an attempt not to feel grief when you're hurt.

Consider for a moment who in your life retaliates. What is your level of trust with that person?

When others catalyze your pain, you can feel incredibly vulnerable to know they have the power to hurt you. Wouldn't it be nice if you couldn't be hurt again? Or, next best, if they hurt you, you'll hurt 'em back. That is the emotional logic behind retaliation. When you retaliate as a boss, you're using power-over. But when you get back at someone or seek revenge, there is always a cost to your integrity and the relationship.

Remember, you get to choose who you want to be in conflict. You can be gentle with your hurt without seeking revenge. You can take care of yourself without doing things that will later cause regret and shame.

Being good at conflict means learning to be with your hurt and your grief without taking action. It means being a friend to yourself, a sweet and kind friend who will hold you in your pain. If this is something that you want, it will take practice. Psychotherapist, author, and somatic activist Resmaa Menakem distinguishes between clean pain and dirty pain. For him, staying with your hurt is clean pain. Dirty pain, on the other hand, happens when you seek revenge. Often, anger is more accessible to feel than hurt. The aggressive impulse often seems more desirable than vulnerability. It convinces you that you'd feel better if you punched that guy in the nose or lashed out rather than be with your own pain.

You have a choice here between clean pain and dirty pain. If you choose dirty pain, perhaps you punch the guy, which might feel good for a moment, but then you'll feel bad and have to deal with a ton of undesirable consequences. If you choose clean pain, you feel your pain without getting aggressive. That's some serious adulting.

Freedom is having an angry or aggressive impulse and not acting on it. You get to be who you want to be. Does not acting feel great in the moment? Not usually. But when you don't have to clean up a mess you made out of anger or revenge, that's sweet!

This level of discernment is a warrior's training. It's more complex to train this way in the short term, but in the long term, with practice, you'll find that it requires less effort—and certainly less cleanup.

When I trained in aikido, I learned that in sparring with your opponent, fundamental respect is always present. You train in gratitude because the other person is allowing you to practice your skill. Instead of viewing the other as an enemy, they're a training partner, a teacher. You transform the attacking energy they bring to you, and you remain connected with them. You remember that the human in front of you wants what you want: dignity, connection, belonging.

Even as you bring them to the mat, you take care not to harm them. Fighting within this framework doesn't mean you don't have boundaries. It doesn't mean you have to transcend emotion somehow or be the Buddha. It means that you respect your humanity enough to respect the humanity of others. In a similar way, you can choose to be a boss who doesn't retaliate.

De-escalating Conflict

It's easier to repair a conflict when it doesn't go too far, and it's easier to stop a thing than to fix a thing. De-escalation is a powerful interruption strategy. To de-escalate, you can call a time-out. Yes, that's exactly what it sounds like. It's the same thing so many of us have used with young children when the energy needs to be taken down a notch. This works for all kinds of conflicts. It's your own personal panic button or emergency brake.

A time-out is a twenty- to thirty-minute break away from an escalating conversation. During the break, each person works to come back to center.

You know you're in an escalating conversation when you feel the heat starting to rise. The tone is getting more agitated. Each person is starting to get triggered.

When you notice that you're in an escalating conversation, first name it: "This is starting to feel heated." Then you can call a time-out. When you call for a breather, you are essentially saying to yourself, "I don't like what I'm feeling, thinking, or doing."

Calling a time-out has everything to do with you and nothing to do with the other person. It comes from the part of you that is grown and wants harmonious work relationships. You don't call a time-out because you think your coworker or employee needs one. You call a time-out because you have lost your center, and you realize that you won't be able to respond skillfully. Time-outs are a gift that you give to yourself.

Five Steps to Calling a Time-Out

1. Use words. Be responsible and communicate clearly. "I am going to take a time-out."

2. Offer reassurance about where you're going and when you'll be back. You don't need to trigger people's abandonment stuff at this moment, so it sounds like this: "I don't like what I'm feeling, thinking, or doing, so I'm taking a break. I'll be back in twenty minutes."

3. Move to a different space.

4. Once you get there, close the door. You can do many things to calm down. Your only job right now is to calm your nervous system, come back to center, and not perseverate on the fight. You've put yourself in a time-out so you can return to the conversation and respond skillfully.

   Here are some things you can do while in time-out:

   - Tense and relax your muscles.
   - Move your big muscles.
   - Take deep cleansing breaths.
   - B.B.O.D.Y.
   - Read something light on your phone. You don't want to be thinking about the fight.

5. When you've calmed down, you return and check in.

If you find that you still need more time once you get back into the conversation, tell the other person you need another twenty minutes. Keep checking in.

Here are things *not* to do while in time-out:

- Perseverate on the fight.
- Think about what you'll say when you get back in the ring.
- Talk to or text someone else about the fight or the person you're fighting with.

To recap, here are the steps to take when conflict happens:

- Slow down.

- If you're escalating or triggered at any point, take a time-out.

- B.B.O.D.Y. Stay with yourself during the conflict, and commit to naming your truth at some point.

- Listen first before you explain.

- Get curious; ask questions. "Tell me more."

- Repeat what you hear, and ask, "What am I missing?" to make sure you're getting it.

- Make repairs if needed.

Making Repairs

Repair means coming to a resolution for the hurt, harm, or misunderstanding that occurred during conflict. Most people don't know how to make a good repair. Unless you came from a really emotionally intelligent family—which, let's face it, most of us did not—you did not learn this skill growing up. If you get good at repair, you'll knock it out of the park as a boss.

It's important to note that repair cannot happen until harm has stopped happening. If you're still fighting, you are not yet ready to repair. The first step is to stop fighting, come back to center, regulate your nervous system, and calm down.

Relationship repair is acknowledging and honoring the experiences of all involved. There are different elements of the repair process and different things you can do to repair.

A repair can include:

- owning your contributions to the conflict

- listening, then acknowledging the impact you've had on someone

- asking for a do-over

- sharing the impact you experienced
- making a good apology (or acknowledgy—more on this concept later)
- making reparations
- reconciling

Repair is not returning to how things were before the conflict. When our feelings get hurt, we often want to get back to the state we were in before we felt bad. We want to feel like we felt before the yucky thing happened. Repair doesn't erase what happened; it doesn't take things back to a state before the rupture. The rupture has undeniably occurred, and to pretend otherwise would be dishonest.

Being able to repair well will sustain your relationships over time. Even in healthy relationships, people can sometimes act poorly in conflict. We yell, say mean things, get critical, get defensive, stonewall. Getting skillful at repair is part of learning to be a great fighter. You may still do unskillful things in heated moments. No one is perfect. But you're always responsible for your behavior, no matter how triggered you get. You'll always have work to do while in conflict. Practicing repair allows you to be human and mess up. The key is that you then get to be gracious about how you own up to it.

Owning Contributions

The first repair technology is owning contributions. This model comes out of the Harvard Negotiation Project. In essence, whenever there is a conflict, each person involved has contributed to it, causing a rupture. The path toward healing starts with you taking inventory of your contributions.

It's so easy to blame the other person and pinpoint all the ways they contributed. It is much harder to sit with, observe, and name your contributions to the rupture. Owning your contributions means you get very honest. You share with the other person all the ways you see you are responsible for the conflict. How did you act or speak in ways you don't feel good about?

As the boss, you're the person with more institutional power, so it's on you to be the responsible one. While your employee may have said and done crappy things, a power dynamic still exists, and with it, a responsibility. You have to be extra careful with that dragon tail. Owning your contributions can feel vulnerable. But you're a pro, since you know that embodied bosses don't shy away from the truth.

It takes trust to own your contributions first, just as listening before speaking does. You're taking a risk and trusting that the other party will receive you. Hopefully they'll meet you halfway, but you don't know that for sure. You don't know how your employee will show up, or whether they have the skills to acknowledge their part. So you get courageous. Explain what you see as your contributions. What did you do or not do that led to conflict? No need to talk yet about your intentions.

Owning your contributions models accountability. It allows your employee to have a different experience of conflict than they have probably had in their life.

Once you have owned your contributions (and invited your employee to do the same if they want to or can), you can acknowledge the impact.

Acknowledging the Impact

Impact means having a strong effect on someone. When you make an impact on someone, you affect them physically, emotionally, or both. You don't have to agree with someone's experience in order to acknowledge impact. They say, "Ouch, I got my feelings hurt." You say, "I acknowledge your feelings are hurt," regardless of whether it was your intention to do so. You are listening to what they share and validating it.

Both parties usually experience impact during the conflict. But when a power differential exists, one party can experience more impact and harm. In conflict, young children feel a more significant impact than parents. The same is true for employees and bosses.

Initiating a conversation to understand your impact sounds like this: "Hey, tell me the impact you experienced. Let me understand it." Once they have explained, you repeat it back like this: "What I'm hearing you say is [state your understanding of the impact]. Is this how I impacted you?" To acknowledge impact, you must first listen to what that person is sharing. Ask clarifying questions to understand better how your words and actions made an impact on them.

When you ask an employee to share the impact they experienced, you're making a tremendous ask. You're asking them to trust that you will listen and not hold it against them if they're honest. To honor this trust, you must not retaliate, minimize, or get defensive.

You may not be at the point where you trust yourself not to do these things. The only way forward here is to practice. If you don't yet trust your skills, set a boundary with yourself that you will only listen and reflect what you heard. Then, take the time you need to process before coming back to the table with a response.

Listening when someone shares their impact with you can be rough. You may feel blamed or misunderstood, or you may believe that what they share is untrue. For example, you say, "Hey, let me know how you're impacted." Your employee replies, "Well, you did this and this and this," and you're thinking, *No, I didn't do that,* or *No, that's not what happened.* Sometimes the person doesn't have all the information, and your impulse is to let them know. But now is not the time to get into a fight about reality, about whose truth is the absolute truth. If you find yourself getting defensive, name it: "Okay, I want to hear you, and I notice I'm getting defensive. Can we take a brief pause so I can be present and listen?"

When you acknowledge impact, you're saying, "That was your experience; that happened to you. You felt like that." You don't need to defend yourself against someone's experience of impact. Their experience is true to them, but that does not make it objective truth. The impact is their feelings, perceptions, and interpretations. You can listen to something an employee shares, even if you feel defensive about what is "true."

Perhaps you notice your employee is quiet and withdrawn. You ask them what's up. They share their impact with you: "I felt really upset when you didn't respond to my email asking for a raise. I felt petrified I was going to lose my job."

Maybe you didn't even receive that email, or maybe you were planning to talk with them at your meeting next week. Your first instinct might be to respond with, "Why would you think that? That's ridiculous. You're not going to lose your job." If you do respond in this way, you convey the message "You didn't experience that." You aren't acknowledging the impact they experienced. A better response is, "I hear you felt scared when

I didn't respond to your email. That totally makes sense. Let's talk about your salary at our meeting next week."

When someone shares an impact with you, mentally note their exact words. After they finish, ask if you can reflect what you heard. Try to say it exactly in their words. Don't paraphrase, embellish, or interpret. Remember how important being listened to is? Using someone's exact words lets them know how closely you were listening. This is not the time to share any of your thoughts or feelings.

Acknowledging the impact allows someone to have the experience they had, whether or not you agree with it, and whether or not it was your experience. It is valid for them, and you can acknowledge that. This is a time to be slow and spacious. Take a break if either of you starts to get amped up again. Speak slowly, allowing each other to digest what is said.

The Do-Over

No one is perfect all the time. We all have moments when we make mistakes and are less skillful. Have you ever said or done something and wished you could take it back and do it over again, but better next time?

The do-over is precisely what it sounds like. It's like having a magic time machine where you can go back and make grounded, skillful choices— ones the person you want to be would make. You hit rewind and do it again, with a better outcome. The do-over is one of my favorite repair technologies, and I've seen it be successful with all kinds of conflict.

In a do-over, you ask the other person if you can rewind and try that again. It works both in the moment or at any point after a conflict. It can even be months later.

Let's look at how it works. Say you notice that you are in an escalating conversation. The other person asks something that lands hard for you. You notice your impulse to defend yourself. Asking the other person to do a do-over sounds like this: "Hey, I'm feeling defensive; let me take a breath. [pause] Would you be willing to ask me that differently? I want to be skillful in how I answer."

If you notice that something you say lands poorly for you or the other person, you can do a self-do-over. It sounds like this: "Oops, I didn't say that very skillfully. I'm on your side, so can I try that again in a softer way?"

You can ask to do it as a gift for both of you: "Hey, would you be willing to do a do-over with me so we can get a different outcome?"

The cool thing about do-overs is that they build trust. Both people in the conflict attempt to be more skillful with each other. Neurologically—this part is super cool—a do-over lays down a second track in your memory.

After my partner and I got married, we had a conflict while on our honeymoon. I couldn't let go of it for weeks afterward, even though I wanted and needed to. Finally, a month later, I asked, "Hey, would you be willing to do this over?" I told him the outcome I wanted us to create, and he was willing to try.

We role-played the scenario. It took five weeks of fretting about it, but the do-over itself took five minutes. Now I have two memories—the situation as it went down the first time, and the do-over with the outcome I wanted. I get to choose where to place my attention: on the do-over. My partner's willingness to do it again took away the ouch.

It might sound silly, but I promise you that this is an effective strategy. I do this all the time with my kid. Whenever I mess up as a parent, I'm like, "You know what, I wish I had said this to you differently. Can I try saying it to you again?" It's super helpful, it lets me be accountable, and it builds trust between us.

Imagine saying something to an employee that you regret, either in the moment or later. Now imagine approaching them with this: "Hey, I didn't like how I said [that thing] to you. I would like to try in a better way, if you're available for that." How would you respond if a boss came to you like that?

The do-over is not a part of every repair process in the same way owning contributions and acknowledging the impact are. It's not applicable in every situation, but it's a tool in your toolkit that you can pull out as needed. Not every conflict needs to be replayed, but the ones you can't let go of usually do. The do-over can profoundly change your relationships. No one can be skillful in every moment, but with the do-over, you don't have to be.

The Apology and the Acknowledgy

We've talked about owning contributions, acknowledging impact, and do-overs as repair technologies. Let's dive into another great one: apologies and acknowledgies.

As we've discussed, owning your contributions and acknowledging the impact someone experienced are the first part of a good repair. The apology and acknowledgy come after those have happened. Many people try to skip over owning and acknowledging and get right to the apology, but that rarely works.

Apology

Often, what people think they want in order to resolve the conflict—what you've been taught to want—is an apology. An apology is an admission of guilt, a plea for forgiveness, a statement that "I will never do that again."

The problem with apologies is that most people don't know how to do them right. You see this on social media and in the celebrity world every day. Someone is called out, and then they write an apology, but the apology makes it worse.

A good apology acknowledges the harm that occurred and consists of several sequential elements:

- identifying who caused the harm and who gets the apology
- acknowledging the details of what happened
- acknowledging the impact of what happened to the victim; validating that what happened was not okay
- a promise not to repeat that behavior

There is so much that goes wrong in apologies:

- vague or incomplete acknowledgment: "I'm sorry I upset you."
- questioning whether harm happened: "If I hurt you, I'm sorry."
- passive voice: "Mistakes happened." "Mistakes were made." instead of "I did it."
- not showing deep, painful regret that is part of guilt when you do something wrong

In an apology, you accept fault and express regret simultaneously:

- "I'm sorry I said _____."
- "I'm sorry I did _____."
- "I feel bad that I spoke harshly."

- "I feel bad that I didn't email you back on time."

- "I'm sorry I hurt you."

An apology says, "I recognize I impacted you and will try hard not to do that again."

In an apology, you need to show regret, remorse, and humility. These are things that the other person needs to see that you are feeling—your affect. Your vulnerability, sincerity, and authenticity are essential parts of an apology.

It can be scary to see that someone who hurt you lacks remorse for it. If a person who wronged you doesn't feel bad or can't admit they've done something wrong, it can make you lose all trust. If someone can't express that they feel bad about something they've done, it's usually because they feel shame. Don't double down on your harmful behavior because you're afraid to admit you made a mistake.

It takes time to change behavior patterns, so if you find yourself doing the harmful thing again, acknowledge it. You can name that you are there again and that you recognize it: "Oh crap, I'm working on this. But I backslid. I'm going to seek support for this behavior. I'm committed to changing it."

If you apologize—"Oh, sorry I'm late again"—and there's no action behind it, you're not making an effort to change your behavior. When you apologize for something, it's crucial that you commit to doing better. Otherwise, your apology is empty at best and manipulative at worst.

Acknowledgy

When I taught elementary school, I had a student who taught me about the acknowledgy.

Mark was a nine-year-old boy who had had a rough life and had been through some serious stuff. He was charming and the sweetest kid, but he was also a troublemaker. He wasn't super clever about his antics, so he would frequently get caught when he was up to something. I would say, "Mark, I know you cheated on that test; I know you copied somebody else's answer."

He would take a breath, square his shoulders, and then look me right in the eye and say, "Yep, I did that." It was so disarming because he was super sincere. He accepted full responsibility, and he admitted the truth of the situation. Years later, when my somatic coach used the word "acknowledgy," I thought of Mark.

When you acknowledge, you don't:

- minimize
- deny
- pretend
- gaslight

You're like, "Yep, that happened, I did that." You don't depart from yourself or beat yourself up. You remain connected to your inner goodness and acknowledge, "Yep, I did that."

When people think they want an apology, they often want an acknowledgy. An acknowledgy validates someone's experience by agreeing with them: "Yes, that happened." "Yes, I did that." This is especially true for folks who have a history of having their experiences denied or minimized. Instead of jumping to apologize, you can ask your employee what they need. Do they need to hear you say sorry? Or do they just need you to say, "Yep, I did that"?

Reparations

A reparation is something you do to help right a wrong. Sometimes there's nothing you can do to show remorse, but sometimes there is. When that's the case, restorative justice focuses on what you can do to show that you care about the impact you created. This is when you ask yourself, "How can I put action behind my words?" It's important that the reparations you want to make come from an authentic place of wanting to make things right, not from a place of obligation, which can lead to resentment.

It's helpful if the offending party takes the lead in a reparation process. Often we put that emotional work onto the person who received most of the impact. If you approach the person you wronged and say, "What can I do to make it better? Just tell me what you want me to do. Tell me what to say," this request can often feel like yet another burden for the person who received the impact.

One piece of a very thoughtful repair process can look like coming to your employee and saying, "Hey, I understand that this is the impact I caused. I can't take that impact away, but I can demonstrate my commitment to behaving differently. I have come up with some suggestions for reparations. I'm checking in to see if you would like any of these things. You can also let me know if there's something else that would be more helpful."

What Reparations at Work Can Look Like: Meet Lena

At work, reparation can look many different ways. It's about taking concrete, meaningful action and following through. For example, one of my clients, Lena, worked for an online marketing firm. She had risen through the ranks until she was managing a team of graphic designers and copywriters tasked with creating internal marketing materials for a credit card company.

Lena was trained as a designer herself, so she understood the requirements of the job, but she wasn't trained in how to manage others, so she treated her employees as she would have liked to be treated in their shoes. For her this meant giving them a lot of feedback to guide their work, which resulted in them feeling micromanaged and mistrusted.

We started our work together because Lena was receiving feedback from her team and her supervisor that she needed to manage her people more effectively. Lena's somatic shape was contained. She moved through space effectively, but slowly. She sat in my office with her legs pressed together. When I asked how she felt she would often just say "Fine," with no other words to describe her inner world.

As we worked to develop her somatic awareness, she became aware of a felt sense of pressure beneath her sternum. Over time, as she felt herself more, she was able to access pain in her chest. Then one day we had a session where she placed her hand on her sternum, sobbing, because she made contact with the care she had for her team. Lena longed for her employees to feel supported, and she truly wanted to be a caring boss.

We worked together for several months as these longings made themselves known. Lena connected with a desire to show her team she was committed to change and growth, and she pondered what she might do to reestablish trust. The idea of reparations felt exciting to her.

Lena decided to invite each of her employees to join her in separate, private conversations about their experience at work—specifically their experience of her leadership—where they could tell her anything they wanted, and she would listen. She made it clear that it was an invitation, not a mandate. Each of her eight employees agreed. She then asked each of them ahead of time to think of something concrete she could do to help them feel her trust in them. As she listened to each person, she made careful notes of the impact they had experienced and their suggestions for her.

Lena chose to write a statement that would acknowledge her impact. She spent two weeks writing and rewriting a statement that spelled out what she had heard from her employees about the specific impact they had experienced. The statement also included the changes she would be making in response to their feedback, and it asked them to let her know how her new practices were landing.

At the next staff meeting, Lena read her statement and made sure her employees knew they could ask questions or make requests about her leadership going forward.

It took a few months, but at our last meeting, Lena shared that her staff now said they felt she trusted them more, and the team felt more cohesive and collaborative.

There is no model for reparation that will fit every situation. What will be meaningful to each employee is unique to that person. To reiterate, this is not something you do out of guilt. It's something you do to right a wrong. You might offer them a retroactive raise or some extra vacation time; or you could acknowledge your error in public. You can come up with an idea and ask if that, or something else, would feel meaningful.

Caution: do *not* just go ahead and implement a reparation without checking in with them and asking for their feedback first. Doing it that way would make it about you, not about the person who experienced harm. In an employee-centric culture, checking in is essential.

Reconciliation

Reconciliation means coming back to relating to each other. It means letting your guard down and softening with each other. Note that this does not necessarily mean things go back to the way they were before the conflict. Still, reconciliation can be a part of a good repair process. Reconciliation after a conflict is not a given, however. Sometimes relationships need to end, and that's okay.

Reconciliation is a somatic process. When rupture and conflict occur, a trusted employee can feel like an enemy. There's an othering on a very basic somatic level. This can happen even if you completely trust them. Suddenly they're on the outside of your field and the outside of your heart. They're an adversary.

Letting your guard down and feeling safe, connected, and open again is a somatic process. It takes time for your body to relax and unwind. Your brain also needs the data points that come from evidence that both of you are showing up.

If a rupture is like a spiky porcupine, then reconciliation relaxes the quills. Your hackles come down. Your body softens. Again, this can take a while. The best way to move from spiky to relaxed is to have regular daily interactions. Treating your employee like you usually do allows them to relax and both of you to move forward.

Sometimes it becomes clear that it's time to part ways with someone after a conflict. Conflict is a tool of transformation, which can mean a significant change in the relationship. Sometimes it means firing someone. Sometimes it means someone quitting. If you know that an employee has broken your trust in a way that they cannot repair, or vice versa, it's time to say goodbye. In this case, reconciliation does not occur.

When handled well, conflict can be generative. Remaining connected to the humanity of all involved parties is crucial. Repair is an integral part of the cycle of conflict, and through deliberate practice, you can build the skills to do it. If you choose skillful repair as a path, you become a leader in an area where very few are proficient.

Chapter 11 Takeaways

O Conflict requires two people, a disagreement, and the presence of negative emotions.

O Everyone learned how to handle conflict in their family of origin.

O As an adult, you get to decide who you want to be in conflict.

O Conflict can be generative, especially when good repairs happen.

O Don't retaliate; it's not cute.

O Take time-outs while taking care of the relationship. Let people know when you need a break, and when you'll be back.

O There are many good technologies for repairing conflict. You can learn to be excellent at repair.

12

PUTTING IT ALL TOGETHER

SOMATIC LEARNING INCLUDES INTEGRATION. The ideas and practices in this book will only be meaningful if they become a part of you. Being an embodied leader means committing to feeling yourself, from the inside out, every single day. You won't get to a place where you've completely mastered embodiment; there's always more your body can share with you. But your felt sense does become more nuanced, and you become more adept at reading your own cues.

Although helping you create an embodied organization is beyond the scope of this book, I want to leave you with some next steps to take on your somatic work journey.

Deciding you are a person who wants to feel more is a radical move as a boss and as a human. Feeling more means feeling *everything* more, and this is revolutionary in a culture that constantly invites our attention away from what is difficult. Deciding to feel has costs and benefits, as you know. However, speaking both from my experience and that of my clients, I know that feeling matters. Being in touch with yourself makes it possible for you to make choices that will lead to a good life. If you can't feel yourself, it's hard to know what you want.

Perhaps the most significant value you find from practicing embodiment is in your decision-making process. Hopefully, by now you have woven some embodiment rituals into your workday. Consistent practice over time establishes a baseline of felt awareness in your body. And when you feel yourself, clarity is more accessible, which aids in decision-making. Even if you haven't made somatic practice part of your daily life quite yet, you can still consult with your body as you make decisions.

If you face a challenging issue and feel uncertain about which way to move, try this practice: Close your eyes, take a breath, and let go of your thinking. After taking a moment to just be, consider the possible solutions, one at a time. Notice how your body feels in response to each one. Deliberately making your decisions from an embodied place is optimal. Let me be clear: I am not suggesting that you make all decisions based on your feelings alone. But giving yourself space and time to make a conscious gut check can save you a lot of headaches.

If all you learn in this book is how to be more embodied in your life, that will be of incredible value. If you go further and bring these principles and practices to your team, you can create a workplace culture of embodied humanity, where everyone gets to be a learning, growing, mistake-making human, and where everyone thrives. And the ideas in this book are applicable on an even larger scale than that.

It is valuable beyond measure to create work that embraces whole people and allows people's full humanity to show up. As a leader, you are responsible for creating safety for your team. When you encourage open and honest feedback, the quality of your relationships improves. As your relationships improve, your team's output increases. Not surprisingly, this benefits the company's bottom line in the long run. It's common sense, but so many bosses forget it.

When employees feel valued and appreciated, they have ownership, and they give more to the project. Your employees need to know you care about them. They want to care about what they're doing at work because this is how they spend a significant part of their lives. Meaning matters.

Creating a Culture Bosses and Employees Love

Many bosses rely on HR to set an organization's culture, but leaders people love know it is *their* job. You can create any kind of culture you want. The how matters. *How* you are shapes the culture of your company. Is there congruence between your stated values and the actions and practices you engage in? How do you live in your body? How do you communicate and function in relationships? When you mess up, do you demonstrate willingness to be accountable? Paying lip service will not work. Organizational change that sticks relies on you changing and becoming more skillful.

Think about the kind of culture you love working in. Do you like a little friendly competition on the team? Do you like to feel that there is deep care and support? Do you like autonomy? Exuberance? Quiet joy?

Considering how you want your workplace to feel is an excellent place to start. Just as interpersonal relationships have dynamics, companies have vibes. Organizations take on the shapes of their leaders. This means that how you are shapes your organizational culture. You may or may not have a big budget for organizational culture development, but you can make big changes in how it feels at work regardless of your budget.

Instead of trying to create culture around the people you hire, I suggest you deliberately map out the culture that leadership wants. Part of this is knowing what your values and mission are, but those are just the bare bones. Especially if you're just starting a company, know that your company culture will be built around its practices. For example, if you launch a start-up with everyone working fourteen-hour days, working through meals, and sleeping at the office, it will be very difficult to change the culture so it's no longer focused on urgency. If leadership values nonurgency in the culture, you've got to build for that through practices instead of retrofitting later.

When you're clear about what culture you practice, it's easier for potential employees to decide whether your company is a good fit for them, and for you to decide whether they're a good fit for you. For example, if humor is a company value, a very serious and studious candidate will feel ill at ease on your team.

I don't mean to imply here that you shouldn't be sensitive to employees' diverse needs, or that you should only hire people who are exactly like you or who fit a template. Sustainability is fed through diversity. An employee-centric company culture listens to employees and implements changes without losing connection to the central values that anchor the company.

In designing or retrofitting company culture, remember that power dynamics set the tone. They affect how you communicate, how you collaborate, who gets heard, and what ideas get brought to the table (or not). Knowing your values around sharing power allows you to develop practices that create the culture you want.

As you create organizational change, some employees will feel better, and some will become unhappy. As a boss, it is not your job to make everyone happy, but it is your job to listen to your team's thoughts, concerns, and feelings. Not everyone will be a good fit for your workplace. Your workplace won't be a good fit for everyone. That's okay. Part of being an embodied boss is accepting that you won't make everyone happy, and the workplace culture you want to lead may leave some people out.

For example, in my company it was imperative to me that we all felt like we could make mistakes. Some of the most outstanding, serendipitous solutions to complex problems result from what are first seen as mistakes. Mistakes often occur as part of a creative process. For those who have a growth mindset, errors point the way to new learning. At our company, we created a culture of celebrating mistakes. We codified this part of our culture in our HR manual like this:

> Our company views mistakes as crucial to the learning process. Growth becomes possible only when we push our edges and move beyond our comfort zone. We consciously create a culture of celebration of errors for the future attention they bring. Through error, we learn to self-correct.
>
> Whenever possible, you are invited to claim it with pride if you notice you have made a mistake. "Woo-hoo! I messed up!" is a message we love to receive. We are not creating a culture of perfectionism. We are building

a culture that welcomes your humanity and the innovation that occurs when folks get to be human!

We ask that you consider these questions: How was that mistake valuable? What did I learn from it?

Our practice of celebrating mistakes meant asking everyone to share their best mistake in our weekly meeting. When we made a mistake, we messaged everyone on Slack: "Woo-hoo! I just made a mistake!"

I want to work in environments with playful people. I always want to be learning. This is how I want it to feel, so I built the company for that. You get to set the tone for your team. Culture gets created through what people jointly practice. Decide how you want it to feel, then design practices that support that feeling state. Want it to feel fun? Have company practices of joy.

If you want to create an embodied, trauma-informed culture of listening, collaboration, play, and joy, which practices will you put into place to get that result? Culture is the result of *practice,* not just intention. It's your job as the boss to envision what's possible beyond where your organization is right now, and then take action to achieve that vision. Dream a big dream, and then develop a plan to make it come true.

What you commit to practicing defines not only your organization but also who you are as a leader. The ideas in this book will continue to be just words on paper unless you put them into action. Through practicing B.B.O.D.Y. and the other practices laid out in these pages, you can be a leader who is ethical, effective, kind, skillful, loving, and human.

PRACTICE MOMENT: How Do You Want Your Work Environment to Feel?

First, take a moment to B.B.O.D.Y. Then do the following:

- Feel into yourself and let this question land on your body: "How do I want work *to feel?*"

- Let your imagination wander.
- Don't worry about how you'll make it feel that way. Stay with curiosity. What does your heart long for? What kind of work space would feel wonderful?
- Make some notes about your findings.

Getting There from Here

Providing institutional support for feeling is revolutionary. Creating an embodied workplace is a significant undertaking. Although this topic could take up another entire book, you hold the principles in your hands. An embodied culture happens one body at a time.

Your company likely has a vision statement, but it probably is not embodied. Bodies were likely not consulted in the creation of your vision, nor is the vision likely to be put into a somatic practice that can be felt.

Like practices, vision and mission statements need to be living documents that can change to hold the bodies that are holding them.

Do you have a shared understanding of what kind of team you're creating? This would be like a vision statement for your company, but smaller and more personal. To do this, take your notes from the previous practice moment, share them with your team, and use them to craft a statement. It might be something like:

> We are an embodied, empowered, and collaborative team. Our highest value is welcoming the humanity of each of our members while working together toward the shared goal of _____.

It's important for this to be a power-with exercise. If you were to write it on your own and then share it with your team, that would be using power-over.

Remember that what you value, you practice. Your embodied leadership presence is foundational because organizations reflect the bodies of their leaders. If you're chronically stressed and contracted, you'll notice this reflected in your employees and your organization's culture. Your leadership *is* your body. Your words and actions are essential, but *how you are* matters more.

Simply speaking, when you are an embodied boss, that very fact helps to create an embodied workplace. When you as the leader practice attention, presence, consent, boundaries, and listening, your organization is practicing those concepts. You create a culture with those values, supported by practice.

PRACTICE MOMENT: Which Practices Get Your Organization There?

As a final step of this book, let's have you design a practice that supports your organization feeling the way you want it to feel. Let's review the steps to creating a practice from chapter 5, with a shift from the personal to the organizational level.

Steps to create an organization-level practice:

1. Choose a capacity or narrative your organization wants to embody.

2. Decide why that capacity or narrative matters to your culture or mission.

3. How will you know when your organization has embodied that?

4. What is one actionable step you can implement to make that happen?

5. Where and when will this practice happen?

6. When and how will your team reflect on your somatic learning?

7. How will your team celebrate doing this practice?

As an example, let's look at how I applied these steps in my company, based on the story I told you above about creating a culture that celebrates mistakes.

1. New narrative: Mistakes generate creative problem-solving and learning.

2. This narrative matters because we want to be an organization with a growth mindset that honors everyone's humanity and potential as a learner.

3. We'll know we have embodied this narrative when the team isn't hiding mistakes anymore and is openly announcing them.

4. We can write a policy for our HR manual and seek team feedback.

5. We'll acknowledge our mistakes on Slack and in our weekly team meetings.

6. We'll offer a weekly reflection on each team member's best mistake and their learning.

7. When someone announces a mistake, they'll receive celebration and commendation for their courage and their willingness to operate with a growth mindset.

Before you start, do the "Quick Power Fix" practice from chapter 5: Lift up. Widen out. Breathe a full breath.

Now do it! Grab your writing device and brainstorm how you will implement these steps. Allow curiosity and surprise to widen your perspective. Remember, you base the culture you create on how you want to feel. This is not the final process but rather an imaginal experience of what could be—if you practice!

Conclusion

There is no one right way to be embodied. You'll feel your way into what's suitable for you. Steer clear of what I call "the tyranny of embodiment," by which I mean the idea that you must be embodied at every moment. You're learning a new language of sensation and emotion, and that takes time. You won't feel yourself and your perfect embodiment at every moment. There are sometimes excellent and important reasons to move your attention away from feeling—having eye surgery, for instance. Let this process be one of playfulness and curiosity rather than one of shoulds and have-tos. You *get* to be embodied when and how it's right for you.

If you've felt skeptical while reading this book, good! Your dissent and critical thinking are welcome. I encourage you to keep gathering your data. Try the techniques and see what happens. My clients and students consistently report positive results. Now it's up to you to explore the results you'll get from being an embodied leader.

Once I got the hang of my dragon tail, my employees started to say things like, "This is the best place I've ever worked." I don't say this to brag but rather to encourage you to practice. For those who have the resources to get additional professional somatic support, that may be needed at this time. Nothing will change unless you change what you practice. It does take a little while to get good at new things, so keep at it for a year, and notice what shifts.

Welcome your humanity and the entirety of your experience. This helps you bring your vision for leadership into reality. You don't have to go it alone, nor should you. If you were going to learn to scuba dive, you'd take classes and pass a test. While many bosses can be rugged individualists, you will get where you want to be faster with the help of someone trained to guide you there. Reading this book is not enough to create change. My strong suggestion is for you to work with a somatic coach trained in embodied leadership. Your coach can help you live these principles.

While we've come to the end of these pages, your journey is just beginning. Wherever you are in your process of embodied leadership, my wish for you is the same: Feel yourself. Trust yourself. Practice. That is the road to being the boss you long to be. Leadership has been a sacred human role for millennia. Inhabit your skin and embody your power, and you will become the unforgettable leader people love. Now go out there and feel yourself, like a boss!

ACKNOWLEDGMENTS

THE WORK OF OTHER SOMATIC teachers has significantly influenced me.

Working with Master Somatic Coach Meredith Broome changed my life on every level. This book, and many of the teachings it contains, would not exist without her. Meredith was trained by Strozzi Somatics and was an early lead teacher in generative somatics. Thank you, Meredith, for all your love and for teaching me to inhabit the full capacity of my sensations and emotions.

The work of Dr. Peter Levine and Somatic Experiencing has been influential in my understanding of trauma.

I have also learned about attention, intention, and so much embodied wisdom from my friend and mentor Dr. Joseph Kramer.

Barbara Carralas taught me how to feel myself and to explore edges through practice.

Gabrielle Roth and 5 Rhythms is the lineage of embodiment where I have learned cycles and rhythms of energy as they move in the body. Thank you to all my dance teachers, and special thanks to Sylvie Minot.

Everything I know about somatic learning comes from the work of Dr. Maria Montessori and my many students.

Thank you to every single one of my clients over the years, who taught me to be a human in the room with you. The gift of your trust and your rigor of healing are both humbling and powerfully inspiring.

This book draws on many years of exploring power and communication in two consensus-based groups, Reclaiming Free Cascadia Witch Camp and the Embodiment Arts Collective, both now ended but great sources of learning and wisdom. Many thanks to all of those who sat in endless organizing meetings as we tried to share power with love and responsibility.

My Wellcelium team who kindly stayed with me as I fumbled my way to leadership: Lauren, Laurel, Cat, Asha, Clarissa, and Anthony. Your professionalism and care were epic.

To the fantastic team at North Atlantic Books, thank you for believing in this book. Shayna Keyles, Amy Reed, Brent Winter, Janelle Ludowise, and especially Margeaux Weston, your guidance and commitment to the shine are much appreciated! What a dream come true to work with NAB.

My Miracle-Glo team deserves unending gratitude for showing up every week to make our lives miraculous! You're the sparkle gleaming behind this book!

Thanks to Moona, who slept the deep sleep of the teenaged while I wrote on our Belize balcony overlooking the sea, and to Orione, who taught me what relationship repair feels like.

Deepest gratitude to my Belover Ari, who is there for every dance move on the floor. I love you.

And you, my reader. Thank you for the gift of your time and attention, and your willingness to explore new ways of being and feeling, for the sake of an equitable world.

RESOURCES

BOOKS

Tension & Trauma Releasing Exercises by David Berceli

Mindset: The New Psychology of Success by Carol Dweck

Waking the Tiger: Healing Trauma: The Innate Capacity to Transform Overwhelming Experiences by Peter Levine and Ann Frederick

Nonviolent Communication: A Language of Life: Life-Changing Tools for Healthy Relationships by Marshall B. Rosenberg

NONVIOLENT COMMUNICATION

List of feelings: *https://www.cnvc.org/training/resource/feelings-inventory*

List of needs: *https://www.cnvc.org/training/resource/needs-inventory*

SOMATIC MODALITIES

- EMDR
- generative somatics
- Hakomi
- Internal Family Systems
- Somatic Experiencing
- Strozzi Somatics

FREE DOWNLOADABLE RESOURCES

The following resources are available on my website (*www.pavinimoray*
.com/bonus.html):

- B.B.O.D.Y. cheat sheet
- Recorded guided grounding meditation

REFERENCES

Berceli, D. *Trauma Releasing Exercises (TRE): A Revolutionary New Method for Stress/Trauma Recovery.* Charleston, SC: BookSurge Publishing, 2005.

Boogaard, Kat. "How to Successfully Navigate Power Dynamics at Work." *The Toggl Blog* (blog), September 22, 2022. *https://toggl.com/blog/power-dynamics-at-work.*

Brom, Danny, Yaffa Stokar, Cathy Lawi, Vered Nuriel-Porat, Yuval Ziv, Karen Lerner, and Gina Ross. "Somatic Experiencing for Posttraumatic Stress Disorder: A Randomized Controlled Outcome Study." *Journal of Traumatic Stress* 30, no. 3 (2017): 304–12. *https://doi.org/10.1002/jts.22189.*

Chödrön, Pema. *Fail, Fail Again, Fail Better: Wise Advice for Leaning in to the Unknown.* Boulder, CO: Sounds True, 2015.

Cloke, Ken. *The Crossroads of Conflict: A Journey into the Heart of Dispute Resolution.* Dallas, TX: GoodMedia Press, 2019.

DeGruy, Joy. *Post Traumatic Slave Syndrome: America's Legacy of Enduring Injury and Healing.* Portland, OR: Joy Degruy Publications, 2005.

DiAngelo, Robin, and Alex Tatusian. *White Fragility.* New York: Public Science, 2016.

Dweck, Carol. *Mindset: The New Psychology of Success.* London: Robinson, 2017.

Gentry, William A. *Be the Boss Everyone Wants to Work For: A Guide for New Leaders.* Oakland, CA: Berrett-Koehler, 2016.

Guarino, K., P. Soares, K. Konnath, R. Clervil, and E. Bassuk. "Trauma-Informed Organizational Toolkit." Rockville, MD: Center for Mental Health Services, 2009.

Hamill, Pete. *Embodied Leadership: The Somatic Approach to Developing Your Leadership.* London: KoganPage, 2015.

Harris, Maxine, and Roger D. Fallot. "Envisioning a Trauma-Informed Service System: A Vital Paradigm Shift." *New Directions for Mental Health Services* 89 (2001): 3–22. *https://doi.org/10.1002/yd.23320018903.*

"How to Manage Trauma." National Council for Behavioral Health. Accessed December 5, 2022. *https://www.thenationalcouncil.org/wp-content /uploads/2022/08/Trauma-infographic.pdf.*

Kendi, Ibram X. *How to Be an Antiracist.* New York: Random House, 2020.

Kurtz, Ron. *Body-Centered Psychotherapy: The Hakomi Method.* Mendocino, CA: LifeRhythm, 2015.

Levine, Peter A., and Ann Frederick. *Waking the Tiger: Healing Trauma.* Berkeley, CA: North Atlantic Books, 1997.

McCormick, Jim. *First-Time Manager.* New York: HarperCollins Leadership, 2021.

Ogden, Pat, and Janina Fisher. *Sensorimotor Psychotherapy: Interventions for Trauma and Attachment.* New York: W. W. Norton, 2015.

Olssen, M. C. "Mental Health Practitioners' Views on Why Somatic Experiencing Works for Treating Trauma." MSW clinical research paper, St. Catherine University, 2013. *SOPHIA. http://sophia.stkate.edu /msw_papers/244.*

Parker, Catherine, Ronald M. Doctor, and Raja Selvam. "Somatic Therapy Treatment Effects with Tsunami Survivors." *Traumatology* 14, no. 3 (2008): 103–9.

Porges, Stephen W. *Polyvagal Safety: Attachment, Communication, Self-Regulation.* New York: W. W. Norton, 2021.

Realmuto, G. M. "Shattered Assumptions: Towards a New Psychology of Trauma." *Journal of the American Academy of Child & Adolescent Psychiatry* 33, no. 4 (1994): 597–98.

Richo, David. *Triggers: How We Can Stop Reacting and Start Healing.* Boulder, CO: Shambhala, 2019.

Rosenberg, Marshall B. *Nonviolent Communication: A Language of Life.* Encinitas, CA: PuddleDancer Press, 2015.

Rymut, Julia. "How to Prepare for Meditation: 9 Ways to Ground Yourself." *About Meditation* (blog). March 24, 2016. *https://aboutmeditation.com /how-to-prepare-for-meditation/.*

Salberg, J. "On the Evolution of Witnessing and Trauma Transmission." *Contemporary Psychoanalysis* 51, no. 2 (2015): 185–94.

Shapiro, F. "Eye Movement Desensitization and Reprocessing (EMDR): Evaluation of Controlled PTSD Research." *Journal of Behavior Therapy and Experimental Psychiatry* 27, no. 3 (1996): 209–18.

Starhawk. *The Empowerment Manual: A Guide for Collaborative Groups.* Gabriola Island, BC: New Society Publishers, 2012.

Starhawk. *Truth or Dare: Encounters with Power, Authority, and Mystery.* New York: HarperOne, 2011.

St. Just, A. *A Question of Balance: A Systemic Approach to Understanding and Resolving Trauma.* North Charleston, WV: BookSurge Publishing, 2009.

Stone, Bruce, Sheila Heen, and Bruce Patton. *Difficult Conversations: How to Discuss What Matters Most.* New York: Viking, 1999.

Strozzi-Heckler, Richard. *The Art of Somatic Coaching: Embodying Action, Wisdom, and Compassion.* Berkeley, CA: North Atlantic Books, 2014.

Strozzi-Heckler, Richard. *Holding the Center.* Petaluma, CA: Strozzi Institute, 2016.

Strozzi-Heckler, Richard. *The Leadership Dojo: Build Your Foundation as an Exemplary Leader.* Berkeley, CA: Frog Ltd., 2008.

Van der Kolk, B. A. *The Body Keeps the Score: Brain, Mind, and Body in the Healing of Trauma.* New York: Penguin Books, 2015.

Van der Kolk, B. "How Trauma Lodges in the Body." *On Being,* podcast, hosted by Krista Tippett. July 11, 2013. *https://onbeing.org/programs /bessel-van-der-kolk-how-trauma-lodges-in-the-body-mar2017/.*

Wheatley, Margaret. *Leadership and the New Science.* Oakland, CA: Berrett-Koehler, 2006.

INDEX

ABOUT THE AUTHOR

Photo credit: Leea Gorell

PAVINI MORAY has started, failed, and succeeded at many businesses. A serial entrepreneur, they have built private practices, a worker collective, and a for-profit company. Thirty years of teaching experience has shaped them into a service-oriented leader, facilitator, and teacher who meets students and clients where they are. A somatic coach specializing in trauma and relationships, they have developed pedagogy and methodology for embodied relationships. They have helped thousands live lives of pleasure and satisfaction. Pavini is a queer, trans, nonbinary founder with insight into outsider cultures and the need for accessibility. Moray holds an MEd in Montessori curriculum design, as well as a PhD in somatic psychology. Pavini is available for organizational speaking, consulting and training. Learn more at *pavinimoray.com*.

About North Atlantic Books

North Atlantic Books (NAB) is a 501(c)(3) nonprofit publisher committed to a bold exploration of the relationships between mind, body, spirit, culture, and nature. Founded in 1974, NAB aims to nurture a holistic view of the arts, sciences, humanities, and healing. To make a donation or to learn more about our books, authors, events, and newsletter, please visit www.northatlanticbooks.com.